OUT OF THIN

THE ORIGIN OF SPECIES

SHAWN BOONSTRA

IT IS WRITTEN
INTERNATIONAL TELEVISION

and Pacific Press Publishing Association

Book Design and Layout by Fred Knopper
Cover Design by Palmer Halvorson
Editing by Judy Knopper
Proofreading by Elwyn Platner, Michele Stotz

Additional copies of this book are available by
calling toll free 1-888-664-5573 or visiting
www.itiswritten.com

Printed in the United States of America
by Pacific Press Publishing Association
Nampa, Idaho / Oshawa, Ontario, Canada
www.pacificpress.com

ISBN 10: 0-8163-2245-7
ISBN 13: 978-0-8163-2245-9

CONTENTS

DEDICATION

This is not a science book, even though it *is*, to some small degree, about science and the way it is practiced in the twenty-first century. Many books have been written which cover the disciplines of geology, anthropology, physics and biology from a great number of perspectives, and so there is no need to add to that library at this point. Thousands of volumes, some of which are very thick indeed, have also been written pointing out the scientific problems with the theory of evolution, so there is no need in this book to reiterate all of the many examples in nature that fly in the face of Darwinism.

Rather, this book is rather about questions. Since the beginning of the scientific revolution, many people have expressed their doubts about the existence of God; I also want to express *my* doubts about popular theories of origins, albeit from a different perspective. I wish to unveil the shallow thinking that usually accompanies arguments against the existence of God or the possibility of creation. The existence of God, after all, is the real debate. If He exists, then creation should not be a problem for thinking people.

This book dedicates a great deal of space to some of the philosophical implications of evolutionary theory. Again, much has been written on the debate over origins that covers scientific fields of study like biology, genetics, and astrophysics. Many of the available titles, however, do not explore the serious spiritual, emotional or philosophical implications this debate has had on the average person who must live life with or without a God, depending on his or her perspective. While atheism is often presented as merely a rational approach to life, it has dramatic implications for how we learn to cope with our existence on this planet. Far from being a benign theory or philosophical framework, atheism has done more than its share to contribute to human hopelessness and despair. The human race, now believing that we were born out of thin air without Someone to guide the process, has been forced to live without meaning.

I wish to dedicate this book to my family. My wife and daughters have been very patient as they tiptoed around the house, giving me the space I need to write. The joy they add to my life is also living proof that God is real and our faith did not emerge from thin air.

CHAPTER ONE

Where You Come From Matters

I made a horrific discovery a little while ago. A recurring back injury had flared up and I was forced to spend a couple of days flat on my back, staring at the ceiling while I waited for the excruciating spasms to subside. As I pondered the ceiling in our bedroom, it occurred to me that there was a distinct possibility that I had a claim to Dutch citizenship. Even though I was born in Canada, my father had been a Dutch citizen at the time of my birth.

Fighting a particularly painful spasm, I very carefully rolled over on the bed and grabbed my laptop computer, which had been my sole source of entertainment for the past two days. I wrote a quick e-mail to the Dutch Consulate in Ottawa to see if they could verify my hunch. Two days later the answer came. I was considered a Dutch national until I was twenty-eight years old, at which point my eligibility for citizenship was revoked.

Dutch law says that once a citizen leaves the Netherlands and does not renew a passport or other citizenship documents for a period of ten years, his or her citizenship is lost. I lost my claim on Dutch nationality on my twenty-eighth birthday because that day marked ten years from the age of majority in the Netherlands. Had I walked into a Dutch consulate and asked for a Dutch passport before my twenty-eighth birthday, I would have gotten it.

I phoned my brother, a lawyer in Canada, and told him what had happened. He also sent an e-mail to the consulate, only to receive the same reply. For about two weeks we pursued the possibility of having our lost nationality restored to us, but to no avail. Our Dutch nationality was gone forever. The only way to become a Dutch citizen now would be to follow the same path as anybody else: through the slow process of naturalization.

I can't begin to describe the amazing sense of loss I felt when I realized that my heritage had been taken from me on a technicality. To be honest, the feelings of remorse were a bit of a surprise, because all my life I hadn't known I had a claim to citizenship and had never missed it. Then, a few weeks later, a story ran in the Reuter's news service that really rubbed salt in my wounds. The headline: "Batman's Nemesis, The Joker, Gets His Dutch I.D." The subheadline: "Is the Joker, one of Batman's fiercest enemies, a Dutch citizen?" Apparently, a 35-year-old man in the Netherlands convinced the authorities to issue him an identity card with a picture of himself dressed up as The Joker. Now my sense of loss was heightened: I couldn't have Dutch citizenship, but they had given it to a cartoon character?

Knowing where you come from is important. There's a good reason that the second most popular hobby in America, after gardening, is genealogy. A powerful instinct leads many of us to hyphenate our nationality in North America, referring to ourselves as "African-Americans" or "Dutch-Canadians." If you can figure out where you come from, you might be able to make sense out of where you're headed. If you know where you're headed, you will know what you're supposed to do with your life.

Our heritage as a human race has been stolen from us. And without it, we're not sure what we're supposed to do with ourselves. In my office at home I have an old chart more than twenty feet long that traces the general genealogy of the human race from the time of Adam and Eve right down to the early 1800s. Somebody, with an open Bible on one hand and an open history book on the other, went through great pains to create it. What is most striking about it is the unbroken flow of history that connects ancient Biblical personalities to modern history. There are no significant breaks or historical uncertainties in the flow of the chart. With impressive certainty the modern human race is traced all the way back to the stories mentioned in the Bible.

Most generations that have lived on planet Earth would have little difficulty accepting the authenticity of the chart's history. It is only in recent years that our attitude towards traditional human history has shifted. We no longer accept the stories of the Bible as history. Somewhere along the way somebody drew an arbitrary line in the flow of history and determined that those who come after the line are real historical people; those who came before the line are mythological figures. And while few would dare to suggest that such eminent personalities as Jesus of Nazareth didn't actually exist, most seem to agree that Adam and Eve were not real people. The difficult question, of course, is to determine where you will draw the line in Biblical genealogies to separate "fact" from "fiction." The Bible draws an unbroken line from Jesus all the way back to Adam, naming each member of the family along the way. At what point do we assume that these were not real people? And what evidence do we have that they were not?

Historically we have not fared well when we have questioned the Biblical record. For decades critics scoffed at the Bible's mention of a Hittite tribe in the ancient world, because archaeology had provided absolutely no evidence of their existence. In the face of missing evidence it was assumed that the Bible writers had invented them. (Human beings seem to have a remarkable talent for assuming that what they have not yet experienced personally is not real.) More than a few faces were red, however, when years later archaeologists unearthed unquestionable evidence of the Hittites at a dig in Bogazkoy, Turkey. Other critics used to scoff the existence of a land named "Canaan," until tablets were discovered in Northern Syria that used the name—tablets written hundreds of years before Moses! Still others used to scorn the Biblical mention of an Assyrian king by the name of Sargon, citing a lack of archaeological evidence to try and prove that Bible history was unreliable. They were silenced when Sargon's palace was discovered in Khorasbad, Iraq. And, to make matters worse for the critics, there were records scrawled on the palace walls that verified the story of the capture of Ashdad as found in twentieth chapter of Isaiah.

To date not one archaeological discovery has discredited Biblical history. To the contrary, it seems the more we unearth the more we discover that the Bible has been right all along. So why have so many people worked so hard to discredit it? Why do we seem to have such an overwhelming need to rewrite history?

There are several possibilities. A few years ago I had an opportunity to look at some very old family records that had been gleaned from a church in the Netherlands. Upon close inspection I noticed that someone had tampered with one of the dates of birth; a number had been obliterated with a razor blade and replaced with a different one.

You could still see the faint outline of the original. The reason for the change was obvious: had they retained the original number, it would be obvious to anyone who checked that the baby was born out of wedlock. Because this took place well over a century ago, the parents were desperate to keep their transgression a secret. The solution? Rewrite history and make the baby younger!

Is it possible that some people feel a need to rewrite human history because they find something objectionable in our past? Does the traditional account of our heritage make some people squirm because of the implication it has for our everyday life? If we claim God as our Father, as most of our forefathers did, there is more at stake than the accuracy of a genealogical chart. After all, if we really come from the hand of a Creator God, He might have something to say about the way we live our lives.

There are those who would argue that they are re-evaluating the story of human origins for the sake of uncovering truth. Undoubtedly some of these people are sincere, but I sometimes wonder what the man who painstakingly made the history chart in my study would think of that claim. If the story of human origins is going to be altered so radically, surely there must be a mountain of evidence to support the new family tree.

If we're going to move away from a long line of real names with plausible dates and adopt a multi-branched tree where humans find themselves living at the end of one twig labeled "homo sapiens" in the "primate" section of the tree, there must be a really good reason for doing it. We must have a lot of evidence to replace Adam with single-celled organisms.

But then again, perhaps there are *other* reasons to rewrite human history—reasons that ultimately have little to do with a simple quest for truth. As our ability to study the universe expands, we have been surprised at the complexity we have discovered. We can no longer permit ourselves to think that single-celled organisms are simple. Our microscopes have now uncovered the truth. Cells are complex beyond our wildest imaginations, to the point where it almost seems as if they have the ability to *think*.

Our telescopes have shown us a universe that defies the imagination, and even the Big Bang theory has become disconcerting for evolutionary scientists because it suggests a beginning to the universe.

And, as some have asked, did the laws of physics that make our universe possible exist before that supposed event? How could they if they didn't have physical matter on which to exert their influence? Who or what put them into place so they'd be working when the universe arrived? If *time* is part of the fabric of the universe, as Einstein suggested, does that mean that time didn't exist before the big bang? That would mean that whatever or *who*ever brought the universe into existence would have to be non-material and eternal (existing outside of time).

These are questions that science is not being forced to ask, and that makes some people uncomfortable. Maybe the denial of God has nothing to do with science at all, but with a desperate attempt to keep Him out of our lives. Dr. George Wald, a committed evolutionist who won the Nobel prize for physiology in 1967, and professor emeritus of biology at Harvard, has made a rather startling admission:

There are only two possible explanations as to how life arose; Spontaneous generation arising to evolution or a supernatural creative act of God.... There is no other possibility. Spontaneous generation was scientifically disproved 120 years ago by Louis Pasteur and others, but that just leaves us with only one other possibility ... that life came as a supernatural act of creation by God, but I can't accept that philosophy because I do not want to believe in God. Therefore I choose to believe in that which I know is scientifically impossible, spontaneous generation leading to evolution.[1]

Geneticist Richard Lewontin says something similar:

We take the side of science in spite of the patent absurdity of some of its constructs, in spite of its failure to fulfill many of its extravagant promises of health and life, in spite of the tolerance of the scientific community for unsubstantiated just-so stories, because we have a prior commitment, a commitment to materialism. It is not that the methods and institutions of science somehow compel us to accept a material explanation of the phenomenal world, but, on the contrary, that we are forced by our a priori adherence to material causes to create an apparatus of investigation and a set of concepts that produce material explanations, no matter how counter-intuitive, no matter how mystifying to the uninitiated. Moreover, that materialism is an absolute, for we cannot allow a Divine Foot in the door.[2]

Is it possible that our decision to abandon God and run with Darwin might have little to do with actual scientific evidence, and more to do with personal preference? If this is true, we have committed a terrible crime against coming generations. We have robbed our children of their heritage. We have deliberately hidden their God-given nationality from them. When they discover one day what we have done, you have to wonder how terrible their sense of loss will be.

CHAPTER TWO

Who You Are Matters

Maybe it speaks to our times, but I saw a baby's bib the other day with the phrase, *"Are You My Daddy?"* stenciled on it. It was only a joke, of course, but it underscores an important point. Most of us have an irresistible urge to figure out where we came from, which is why the test-tube baby industry is facing some tough challenges as privacy laws for male donors are coming under careful scrutiny.

In 2005 a 15-year-old boy made headlines because of his determined search to find his biological father. *U.S. News and World Report* tells us that he relentlessly scoured the Internet, searching DNA databases, until he came up with a solid match. He had found his father.

Why do children want to know? In some cases, they're simply looking for information to help them understand a genetic predisposition to certain diseases. But more often than not, they're looking for something more:

Even if the offspring could get a full medical report, it might not be enough. Many children want to fill what they describe as an emotional void created by not knowing their biological fathers or half of their ancestral past. They aren't interested in money (and their mothers signed away their rights to it anyway) or even an ongoing relationship. Finding their fathers is more about understanding a look, a mannerism, similar tastes, a connection. "I see Mom and me, and that's it," says Mary Catherine, a 21-year-old college student who was conceived with donor sperm and is hoping to find her biological father. "It would be wonderful to see that other part—even just to know what he looks like," she says. Now, as the barriers of anonymity are chipped away, it's a picture that many children of sperm donors may eventually be able to piece together.[3]

Finding your father gives you a pretty good chance of figuring out what makes you tick. And figuring out what makes you tick is an important piece of the puzzle when you set out to discover what your life *means*. As it turns out, our greatest need as human beings, once we've been fed and clothed, is *not* love. Love is important, but it's not our most basic need. At the end of the day, what we really want to know is *why* we're here. Is there a purpose for our existence? When we die, will anybody miss us? Will it matter that we lived?

Nothing is quite so bleak as the prospect of discovering that your life is pointless, and so we go to great lengths to figure out what it means. Albert Camus, the French philosopher who struggled so profoundly with the meaning of life, made this observation:

> . . . *I see many people die because they judge that life is not worth living. I see others paradoxically getting killed for the ideas or illusions that give them a reason for living (what is called a reason for living is also an excellent reason for dying). I therefore conclude that the meaning of life is the most urgent of questions.*[4]

Camus was right: the meaning of life *is* the most urgent of questions, and it drives much of our behavior as human beings. It can even cause us to act in an irrational or self-destructive manner.

I'll never forget visiting Patricia in her small one-bedroom apartment. Judging from the pillow and blanket on the love seat, I guessed that she had been sleeping in the living room. A few minutes later, when the bedroom door suddenly swung open, I discovered why.

A rough-looking young man, maybe in his mid-twenties, swaggered into the living room with a young lady hanging off his arm. Both of them were obviously under the influence of something, and when they saw that Patricia had company, they suddenly disappeared back into the bedroom. I understood immediately what was going on.

"Patricia," I said, "are those two people living here with you?"

She nodded *yes*.

"And are you sleeping on the couch because they're using your bedroom?"

"Yes."

"Can I ask you a question?" I asked. "Are they paying you any rent?"

"No," Patricia laughed, half-heartedly. "He says that having his good looks around the apartment is payment enough."

"Is that because he doesn't have any money?"

"Oh, no," Patricia protested, "he has *lots* of money. He's a drug dealer."

I must admit that my temper began to boil when I saw how this lowlife was using Patricia for a free ride. I was just about to offer to physically evict the young man from the apartment when I stopped to ask myself *why* Patricia would allow herself to be used. I quickly looked around the apartment; she didn't have much. I knew something of her family history, and that didn't have much to offer her either. Life had been tough, and I was pretty sure Patricia would have to struggle to give meaning to her life. She needed to be important. She wanted to know that her life meant *something* to *somebody*. And if the only way she could achieve a sense of purpose was to let people take advantage of her, she was willing to be used. She was providing shelter for a social parasite because she derived a sense of meaning (however misguided and minimal) from it.

When we fail to find meaning in our lives, we become prone to simply giving up. There's a reason that those who are attempting to talk someone out of suicide often point to reasons for living, such as the well-being of a spouse or children. They're trying to underscore the idea that the world *needs* them. In the long run, a sense of purpose is as essential to our survival as food and water.

Concentration camp survivor Viktor Frankl brought that lesson home from the Nazi death camps of the Second World War. The SS was particularly adept at stripping prisoners of all sense of self-worth, working them harder than beasts of burden, depriving them of basic nutrition and medical attention, and dehumanizing them in a thousand different ways. Frankl points out in his landmark book *Man's Search for Meaning* that those who had some purpose in life—something to live for—were the most likely to survive.

At one point, the guards discovered that someone had stolen some potatoes, and demanded that the rest of the prisoners give up the culprit or the entire camp would be required to go without food. In spite of the starvation diet they were being forced to live on, the rest of the prisoners—2,500 of them—refused to blow the whistle, even though some of them knew who had committed the offense. Everyone was required to fast, a punishment that drove already low morale even lower. When the lights went out, the senior block warden recognized the danger of having the men in his block sink so far into depression that they would lose all hope. He called on Frankl, a psychiatrist, to give the men a pep talk. Frankl spent his time during the darkness painting a picture of the future, speaking of things that made survival worthwhile:

Then I spoke of the many opportunities of giving life a meaning. I told my comrades (who lay motionless, although occasionally a sigh could be heard) that human life, under any circumstances, never ceases to have a meaning, and that this infinite meaning of life includes suffering and dying, privation and death. I asked the poor creatures who listened to me attentively in the darkness of the hut to face up to the seriousness of our position. They must not lose hope but should keep their courage in the certainty that the hopelessness of our struggle did not detract from its dignity and its meaning. I said that someone looks down on each of us in difficult hours . . . and he would not expect us to disappoint him. He would hope to find us suffering proudly—not miserably—knowing how to die.

And finally I spoke of our sacrifice, which had meaning in every case. It was in the nature of this sacrifice that it should appear to be pointless in the normal world, the world of material success. But in reality our sacrifice did have a meaning. Those of us who had any religious faith, I said frankly, could understand without difficulty. I told them of a comrade who on his arrival in camp had tried to make a pact with Heaven that his suffering and death should save the human being he loved from a painful end. For this man, suffering and death were meaningful; his was a sacrifice of the deepest significance. He did not want to die for nothing. None of us wanted that.[5]

Even when someone else attempts to strip all meaning from our lives, we continue to survive if we can rediscover it. When life at Auschwitz seemed utterly hopeless, and it was certain that many—or most—of Frankl's hearers would never leave the camp alive, many were kept from committing suicide when they were given a reason to live, even if the reason was to face death proudly for the sake of someone who knew them.

Viktor Frankl also points out something eloquently simple and yet remarkably profound: people lose hope when they lose a sense of the future. One of the reasons that concentration camps took such a heavy psychological toll on their inmates was because there was no definite sentence imposed on any them. In a regular prison system, most prisoners have something to look forward to. They have been given a term to serve, and they know approximately how long their present circumstances will last. Concentration camp internees do not have that psychological tool to help them cope. There is no sentence imposed on them, and because a war will last for an indeterminate length of time there is no way for them to set their hopes on something in the future. The future simply doesn't exist, and that perspective (or lack of it) robs prisoners of hope and meaning:

I once had a dramatic demonstration of the close link between the loss of faith in the future and this dangerous giving up. F——, my senior block warden, a fairly well-known composer and librettist, confided in me one day: "I would like to tell you something, Doctor. I have had a strange dream. A voice told me that I could wish for something, that I should only say what I wanted to know, and all my questions would be answered. What do you think I asked? That I would like to know when the war would be over for me. You know what I mean, Doctor—for me! I wanted to know when we, when our camp, would be liberated and our sufferings come to an end.""And when did you have this dream?" I asked.

"In February, 1945," he answered. It was then the beginning of March.

"What did your dream voice answer?"

Furtively he whispered to me, "March thirtieth."

When F—— told me about his dream, he was still full of hope and convinced that the voice of his dream would be right. But as the promised day drew nearer, the war news which reached our camp made it appear very unlikely that we would be free on the promised date. On March twenty-ninth, F—— suddenly became ill and ran a high temperature. On March thirtieth, the day his prophecy had told him that the war and suffering would be over for him, he became delirious and lost consciousness. On March thirty-first, he was dead. To all outward appearances, he had died of typhus.[6]

The lesson was simple: people without a sense of meaning die. Perhaps this has something to do with the unexpected findings of a study on early retirement printed in the *British Medical Journal* in 2005. It turns out that on average, those who opted for early retirement at Shell Oil died sooner than their counterparts who continued working until standard retirement age. Those who chose to retire at fifty-five years of age had a 37 percent higher risk of death at age sixty-five than their counterparts who actually waited until sixty-five years of age to retire. The study also revealed that those who retire at fifty-five are 89 percent more likely to die in the ten years after retirement than those who retire at sixty-five.

Other studies have also shown that retirement tends to bring on earlier death. I can only speculate, but I ask myself the question: does this have anything at all to do with a lost sense of purpose?

While a clear vision for the future and a sense of direction in life are important for our well-being, a sense of our past is also important, because our past reveals who we are. How are we supposed to know what our purpose in life is if we don't know who we are? In Western civilization we have largely let go of our belief in a Creator God, and at the same time we have lost our grip on the past. We are no longer certain of who we are as human beings, and so discovering a meaningful reason for our lives has become a rather difficult task. The sense of loss I felt when I realized I had lost my Dutch nationality was merely irritating; the consequence of the entire human race losing its sense of identity is devastating.

Let's compare two different philosophies of life to illustrate the fundamental change we have undergone in western civilization. The first example comes from the *Westminster Catechism*, a statement of faith that provides a theological framework for millions of Presbyterian Christians. Here is the first question and answer given in the catechism:

Q. What is the chief and highest end of man?
A. Man's chief and highest end is to glorify God, and fully to
enjoy him forever.

Notice the simplicity of this statement of faith: our lives have a purpose, and we know what it is. For thousands of years nobody questioned this kind of thinking. God created us, and we exist for the purpose of having a relationship with Him. When we create something, it is because God is a Creator and we were made in His image. When we love somebody, it is because God is love and we were made in His image. When we achieve great things in our life, it is a monument to the goodness glory of God. Modern thinking, stripped of its belief in a personal God, has robbed us of this essential sense of purpose.

Our second exhibit comes from *The Gay Science*, a book written by Friedrich Nietzsche, the famous nihilistic philosopher from Germany:

Have you ever heard of the madman who on a bright morning lighted a lantern and ran to the market-place calling out unceasingly: "I seek God! I seek

God!" As there were many people standing about who did not believe in God, he caused a great deal of amusement. Why? is he lost? said one. Has he strayed away like a child? said another. Or does he keep himself hidden? Is he afraid of us? Has he taken a sea voyage? Has he emigrated?—the people cried out laughingly, all in a hubbub.[7]

Before you read any further, I should probably offer a word of explanation. Nietzsche believed that human civilization is in the process of discovering that its belief in God was wrong. More specifically, he believed that we are discovering that a belief in God didn't provide a reasonable base for determining our actions or establishing a reliable moral code. The "madman" in this famous passage had come to the realization that Western civilization had lost its grip on a belief in God, and was horrified when he realized what that would mean for future generations. Let's continue:

The insane man jumped into their midst and transfixed them with his glances. "Where is God gone?" he called out. "I mean to tell you! We have killed him, you and I! We are all his murderers! But how have we done it? How were we able to drink up the sea? Who gave us the sponge to wipe away the whole horizon? What did we do when we loosened this earth from its sun? Whither does it now move? Whither do we move? Away from all suns? Do we not dash on unceasingly? Backwards, sideways, forwards, in all directions? Is there still an above and below? Do we not stray, as through infinite nothingness? Does not empty space breathe upon us? Has it not become colder? Does not night come on continually, darker and darker? Shall we not have to light lanterns in the morning? Do we not hear the noise of the grave-diggers who are burying God? Do we not smell the divine putrefaction?—for even Gods putrefy! God is dead! God remains dead! And we have killed him!

How shall we console ourselves, the most murderous of all murderers? The holiest and the mightiest that the world has hitherto possessed, has bled to death under our knife—who will wipe the blood from us? With what water could we cleanse ourselves? What lustrums, what sacred games shall we have to devise? Is not the magnitude of this deed too great for us? Shall we not ourselves have to become gods, merely to seem worthy of it? There never was a greater event—and on account of it, all who are born after us belong to a higher history than any history hitherto!" Here the madman was silent and looked again at his hearers; they also were silent and looked at him in surprise.[8]

Nietzsche was not trying to say that God Himself was biologically dead; he didn't even believe in God. Rather, his point is that the western world was putting its concept of God to death, and in the voice of the madman, you can catch a sense of the despair that Nietzsche himself later felt when he realized that a universe without God is a universe without meaning.

His biggest struggle from that point on was to find a reason to live, and he feared what would happen to civilization should it lose its sense of purpose. He predicted that the twentieth century would be one of the bloodiest in history; he was absolutely right.

This point of view is known as nihilism, the belief that our existence has no real meaning. It forms the basis of Douglas Adam's *Hitchhiker's Guide to the Galaxy* (which has been, in its various incarnations, a radio program, a series of books, and a movie), in which the main characters are on a quest to discover the meaning of life. When a massive supercomputer is asked to consider this question, it contemplates for many years and then spits out the answer, "forty-two." The message Adams is trying to convey? Life is utterly meaningless. Don't bother looking for meaning; you're not going to find any.

Now consider the two examples again. The *Westminster Catechism* gives us a simple but elegant purpose for human life. The other is saturated with angst over the prospect of a universe without God and the meaninglessness of life. Ask yourself which one more closely answers the inherent need we have as human beings to find meaning. If there really is no meaning to the universe, then why do we crave it so much? Why would we have such a strong need for meaning if does not exist?

The theory of evolution cannot answer this question. Our need for meaning would not naturally evolve in a world where there is no meaning to be found. It makes no sense to crave it if we are simply the products of a biological accident that took place billions of years ago. You might be able to explain why we crave food or shelter, but you can't explain why we crave things like meaning and purpose.

If, on the other hand, you consider the possibility that we came into being as the result of the deliberate act of a Creator, and you accept the premise that we were made in His image, you begin to answer the question of why we exist. We are not meaningless organisms—unhappy accidents—hurtling through space on a tiny blue marble we have labeled Earth. Somebody wanted us here:

You are worthy, O Lord, to receive glory and honor and power; for You

created all things, and by Your will they exist and were created."
(Revelation 4:11)

While this one simple statement is likely not enough to satisfy many people's curiosity about our origins, at least it states a clear purpose for our existence. God willed us. He has a reason for us to be here.

The theory of evolution, on the other hand, comes up empty. There is no reason for anything. The big bang just happened. The evolution of intelligent life just happened. And none of it happened for any particular reason. One of our most essential needs—our quest for meaning—can never be satisfied. It's no wonder that Nietzsche lost his sanity and became a madman himself. And it's no small wonder that most people, having been stripped of their historical heritage, struggle with a dark sense of futility. We have come to the point where we are forced to invent a meaning for life, and most of our inventions have failed.

The Nazis grasped at the absurd ideal of a "super man," and a "master race" to give them meaning. They came up with Auschwitz. Many modern North Americans have slipped into thoughtless hedonism, attempting to satisfy every craving their body produces, but failing to answer the question of *why.*

We now behave like people who have no purpose in life. We look for fulfillment in strange places. We eat and drink ourselves to death. We seek satisfaction in meaningless sexual relationships. We spend a significant percentage of our lives in front of a television set, pursuing amusements instead of accomplishments. In short, we have become exactly what the new history charts in our high school textbooks say we are: mere organisms. Our existence has been reduced to the level of machines, performing pre-programmed functions, but without any real meaning.

It is important to understand that this was not true with the vast majority of our ancestors. They had a sense of purpose, even when times were tough. They studied their origins, and as a result, they knew who they were. And that kind of knowledge gave birth to the American experiment and documents like the *Declaration of Independence.*

We hold these truths to be self-evident, that all men are created equal, that they are endowed by their Creator with certain unalienable rights, that among these are life, liberty, and the pursuit of happiness.

We used to govern our behavior by the knowledge of who we were. Children of a Creator God are able to figure out what they should do with their lives. Our ancestors knew they should not behave like animals, because we are children of God. Today we have reversed our logic. Instead of figuring out who we are and governing our behavior accordingly, we now study our behavior—no matter how offbeat or unusual it might be—and we use it to define who we are. And if we behave like animals, we have decided that must be what we are.

CHAPTER THREE

Arguments Against the Existence of God

Number One: The Lack of Evidence

At the foundation of the creation/evolution debate (and the real issue at stake) is the question of God's existence. Some people might find the title of this chapter a little strange, especially when you consider this book was written by a Christian minister, but there is a method to my madness. Hundreds (maybe thousands) of books have been written to expound on the various arguments for God's existence, and I fully intend to discuss some of those arguments. Yet I feel that many Christians operate in a defensive mode, desperately attempting to shore up an argument for the existence of God when the burden of proof appears to fall as much on those who deny the belief that has been a critical part of human existence since time immemorial.

Those who have strongly questioned God's existence have actually done believers a favor, because the questions have required them to be thoughtful and reasonable about their faith. Many generations ago, the Apostle Peter counseled us to "be ready to give a defense to everyone who asks you a reason for the hope that is in you." (1 Peter 3:15) Proponents of Darwinian evolution have forced us to follow the apostle's advice and hone our apologetic skills.

Those who argue that the vast majority of us who continue to believe in a personal God are mistaken, however, should likewise be required to reflect on their arguments and weigh their validity. The arguments offered to disprove the existence of God generally fall into one of five broad categories, which I will discuss in a moment. Before we examine them, however, it is probably important to define at the outset what we mean by "God," because the debate over His existence has often been muddied by various definitions of who or what God actually is. Students of religious philosophy will have to forgive my somewhat oversimplified set of definitions:

(a) **Theists** believe in a personal, intelligent God who still intervenes in the affairs of this world. This is the God of the Bible.

(b) **Deists** believe in an "absentee landlord," a God who created the world but has had nothing to do with it since creation. He is the Master Designer, but He does not hear or answer prayers, or speak to us through divine revelation, etc.

(c) **Pantheists** believe that God is synonymous with everything we see around us. He is merely the personification of nature, a concept used to describe the universe itself (along with its presumed order and meaning).

For the purposes of this book we will use the word "God" in the sense that *theists* use it: the personal God of the Judeo-Christian Bible. This is an important distinction to make, because some people, not understanding the various schools of thought on the nature of God, have leapt to unwarranted conclusions. For example, consider the following statements commonly attributed to the great physicist, Albert Einstein:

Before God we are all equally wise—and equally foolish.

At any rate, I am convinced that He [God] does not play dice.

I want to know God's thoughts; the rest are details.

At first glance, it's tempting to think that Einstein believed in God. The only problem with that conclusion is that Einstein defined God differently than most people. He more or less used the word "God" to describe the majesty of the universe rather than the personal Judeo-Christian God of the Bible. This becomes abundantly clear when you compare the above statements with ones like this:

I do not believe in a personal God and I have never denied this but have expressed it clearly. If something is in me which can be called religious then it is the unbounded admiration for the structure of the world so far as our science can reveal it.

I believe in Spinoza's God who reveals himself in the orderly harmony of what exists, not in a God who concerns himself with the fates and actions of human beings.

Einstein's definition of God was clearly not theistic, which is why those who claim Einstein as a believer are only partially correct. If we want to explore the issues involved in the debate over evolution and creation, we need to be careful about our definitions. A Darwinian, for example, might concede the point that God exists if we define God as the universe itself. He or she will not object to an impersonal God that is nothing more than a scientific principle or a poetic way to describe the grandeur of the universe. The moment you define God as the personal Deity of the Bible, however, they have an objection, because for the most part, evolutionists do not believe in a personal God who deliberately created the world in six days. This God—the One who intervenes in the affairs of men—they cannot bring themselves to accept. There are five basic categories of arguments against the existence of God. Let's examine each of them in turn.

The Argument from a Lack of Evidence

This argument is very simple: where is the evidence of God's existence? If there really is an infinite God who created the universe, shouldn't we see abundant evidence of His existence? If God is real, why doesn't He just show Himself or work a few spectacular miracles like the ones we read about in the Old Testament?

It should be pointed out that sometimes people are willfully ignorant of evidence they do not wish to see. When coalition forces entered the city of Baghdad and captured Saddam Hussein's palace in 2003, Iraqi Information Minister Mohammad Said Sahhaf publicly denied that it had happened. Although video footage clearly showed coalition tanks in the capital, he held an impromptu news conference to declare that people "should not believe these invaders and these liars. There are none of their troops in Baghdad." It wasn't a case of the minister being misinformed; he was denying the obvious in the face of overwhelming evidence. He *chose* not to see the tanks.

Likewise, some people simply *choose* not to see any evidence of God's existence. There is an abundance of natural evidence (some of which we will examine later on in the book) to suggest the existence of a Divine Creator. To suggest there is *no* evidence generally means that one (a) hasn't really looked for any, or (b) is choosing to ignore what is there.[9] Some might argue that they are not completely persuaded by the evidence, or that they personally find it weak, but they cannot argue there is *no* evidence at all.

The question of miracles is one that many people have asked themselves after reading the accounts of great miracles in the Bible.

If the God of the Bible is real, and the miracles that took place in the Bible are also real, then why don't we see more of them in modern life?

To claim that God does not exist because you haven't seen a miracle is a little like a dog denying *your* existence because you didn't arrive home at the expected time to fill his dog dish. For the most part your dog is not able to comprehend *why* you might have had other priorities at the time. He might not have seen you putting out the fire in the field next door so that the house wouldn't burn, or he might not have seen you discovering that the dog food was infested with vermin and running to the store for a new supply. Dogs don't comprehend our motives because they operate on a lower mental plane than we do.

Much of our disappointment with God comes from our expectation that He will act like a human being, with our priorities and on our schedule. Even though the Bible teaches that God is *like* us (or more accurately, we are like Him), we are nevertheless greatly dissimilar. A passage found in the book of Isaiah makes this abundantly clear:

"For as the heavens are higher than the earth, so are My ways higher than your ways, and My thoughts than your thoughts." (Isaiah 55:9)

Another passage from the book of Ecclesiastes makes the same point using different language:

When I applied my heart to know wisdom and to see the business that is done on earth, even though one sees no sleep day or night, then I saw all the work of God, that a man cannot find out the work that is done under the sun. For though a man labors to discover it, yet he will not find it; moreover, though a wise man attempts to know it, he will not be able to find it.
(Ecclesiastes 8:16, 17)

Let's face it: if God is real, and the Bible's description of Him is accurate, you're not going to be able to fully wrap your finite mind around the concept. After all, He is described as infinite and omniscient, and we are both finite and severely limited by the vast body of knowledge we don't possess. Admittedly, it hurts our intellectual pride to consider that there are things we may not be able to discern through simple human logic, but how and when God chooses to act would certainly fall into that category.

My two daughters don't always understand *my* behavior. They don't understand why I don't want to get out of bed at 6 a.m. on a holiday.

They can't comprehend why I don't want to go to McDonald's twice a day. They don't see any good reason why I won't let them stay up all night and watch television unsupervised. And that's because they're children and they have a different set of priorities than I do. They haven't lived long enough or had enough life experience to figure out why certain things are important to me as an adult. That, of course, will change as they mature. In the words of the Apostle Paul:

When I was a child, I spoke as a child, I understood as a child, I thought as a child; but when I became a man, I put away childish things. For now we see in a mirror, dimly, but then face to face. Now I know in part, but then I shall know just as I also am known. (1 Corinthians 13:11, 12)

From our childish point of view, it's difficult for us to understand why, given the prevalence of doubt in this world, God doesn't simply part the clouds, show Himself, and say a few words. If only He would part the Atlantic this time instead of the Red Sea, everybody would believe! Right?

Maybe.

Biblical history demonstrates quite clearly that miracles aren't always a home run for faith. The Israelites witnessed the plagues that fell on Egypt and they saw the Red Sea parted; weeks later they were fearfully complaining that God was going to let them starve to death. And then in the New Testament, Jesus makes a point in one of His parables that shouldn't be missed:

"Then he said, 'I beg you therefore, father, that you would send him to my father's house, for I have five brothers, that he may testify to them, lest they also come to this place of torment.' Abraham said to him, 'They have Moses and the prophets; let them hear them.' And he said, 'No, father Abraham; but if one goes to them from the dead, they will repent.' But he said to him, 'If they do not hear Moses and the prophets, neither will they be persuaded though one rise from the dead.'" (Luke 16:27-31)

In this important parable, a man who discovers that his life was an utter waste and finds himself lost, begs God to let Lazarus rise from the dead to go and warn his family not to follow in his own foolish footsteps. "Lord," he says, "if someone rose from the dead, then they'd believe it!" Jesus' answer is very important: *they already have the scriptures.*

In other words, there is already enough evidence to lead you to God in the scriptures *without* the need for dramatic miraculous phenomena. If you can't find evidence for God in an honest look at the scriptures, it's quite likely you're not going to find it in the spectacular either. Those who ignore the abundance of material already provided by God and demand to see a "magic trick" instead are a little reminiscent of the Iraqi Information Minister demanding more evidence of an invasion when American soldiers are already using the shower in Hussein's palace and his statue is lying toppled in the streets.

During Jesus' earthly ministry the scribes and the Pharisees continually challenged His status as Messiah, and at one point they asked Him to perform a miracle to prove Himself:

Then some of the scribes and Pharisees answered, saying, "Teacher, we want to see a sign from You." (Matthew 12:38)

It's important to remember that when they asked their question Jesus had already performed a number of important miracles. Water had been changed into wine. A paralyzed man had picked up his bed and walked. The daughter of a local ruler had been brought back to life. Sight was restored to the blind, speech was restored to the mute, and scores of sick people were restored to health. The Pharisees had no shortage of miracles to help them see God at work through Jesus. Yet they deliberately chose *not* to believe—which is why Jesus gave them this answer:

But He answered and said to them, "An evil and adulterous generation seeks after a sign, and no sign will be given to it except the sign of the prophet Jonah. For as Jonah was three days and three nights in the belly of the great fish, so will the Son of Man be three days and three nights in the heart of the earth. (Matthew 12:39, 40)

On another occasion, Herod the king brought a group of sick people into Jesus' trial and demanded that He heal them for the king's entertainment. Of course, nothing happened. As you might expect (if you really think about it), God does not jump to attention when human beings demand it. Does He reveal Himself? Yes. Does He answer prayer? Yes. But not unconditionally.

Sometimes atheists approach the subject in a rather childish manner. On occasion, prominent atheists will refer to Christians as "unsophisticated" or "simple" as a way of demeaning their belief system. I'll be the first to admit that sometimes Christians speak before they think, or quickly leap on urban legends to "prove" their faith. But it should also be pointed out that atheists can be equally simplistic when it comes to the matter of understanding scripture.

A while ago I found a stunning example of an atheist's shallow understanding of spiritual principles posted on his website, which was dedicated to ridiculing Christians. At one point he levels this challenge at believers:

Christians—here is an unambiguous, no-catch, 100%, concrete way to prove the existence of your divine being. A way for you to prove without any doubt whatsoever that your God, the Christian God of the Bible, does in fact exist.

If we examine the Christian Holy Bible we discover that a listening God answers prayer and that even the smallest amount of faith can move mountains. Here is my proposition—Pray for me. Pray for me to 'come to God'. Pray for me to accept Jesus. Get your friends to join in, start a prayer crusade for my soul. If you go to church, tell the priest and get him to ask the whole congregation to pray for me. If you are a Christian head-teacher of a Christian school ask the whole school to pray for me at assembly every morning for a week. Post as many notes as you can on your favourite Christian websites to help propagate the cause, or e-mail all your Christian compatriots and ask them to join in. Flood Christian message boards and newsgroups. Write a special prayer and publish it. Spread the word, Martin J. Burn—The English Atheist—is prepared to be changed, by the power of prayer and the power of God, into a good God fearing Christian.[10]

Predictably, this online atheist reports that he has *not* been converted, God is *not* answering the prayers of believers, and therefore God must not exist. This kind of challenge makes it clear that Mr. Burns has not taken the time to examine the basic principles of Christianity laid out in the Bible.

In essence, he's approaching the subject the same way the Pharisees approached it with Jesus: without a shred of sincerity. He has already made up his mind that nothing is going to happen, and he conveniently ignores the fact that God will not force him into the kingdom of heaven against His will.

Let's think it through for a moment. Let's suppose that God *did* force an atheist into the kingdom of heaven against his will. Would the atheist then have a valid complaint against the character of God? Some years ago, my good friend Henry Feyerabend came up with a brilliant illustration of the problem.

One day, a man boarded a ferry that was going to take him to an island where he could spend the day in drunken debauchery and gambling. When he boarded the boat and it pulled away from the dock, he discovered, to his dismay, that it was loaded with happy school children who were cheerfully singing Bible songs. Their "noise" started to irritate him, so he went to the captain to see if he could get him to silence the children.

"Are you kidding?" he said, "tell those kids to be quiet? They're on their way to the Methodist Sunday School picnic, and they're excited. It's the biggest event of the year!"

"What do you mean, Sunday School picnic? I thought this ferry was taking us to the casinos!"

"Oh, no," the captain said. "That's another boat! You're on the wrong ferry!"

The man began to panic. "You've got to turn this tub around!" he cried. "I can't go to a Sunday School picnic!"

"No such doing," said the captain. "I can't alter course."

"But when do you come back?" asked the desperate drunkard.

"At the end of the day."

The man spent one of the most miserable days of his life listening to Bible stories and watching happy children singing and doing various arts and crafts. He hated every minute of it. The children loved it. What was the difference? The children *wanted* to be there.

Now, suppose God was in the business of forcing peoples' hands. How happy is the secular humanist going to be in the kingdom of heaven? Heaven would be misery.

God simply doesn't force the human will. If Martin Burn doesn't *want* to be a Christian, no amount of prayer is going to make it so, because God will not rob him of his free will. If you end up in the kingdom of heaven, it's going to be because you *want* to be there. That's why God continually pleads with us to choose the wise path, instead of cramming a bit in our mouths and forcing us there.

Why doesn't God just *show Himself?* I have to admit that there have been moments when I wished for the same thing—if only for the sake of silencing the critics. But the Bible indicates that's not how God wants things. He wants to be *sought after.*

...so that they should seek the Lord, in the hope that they might grope for Him and find Him, though He is not far from each one of us. (Acts 17:27)

Seek the Lord while He may be found, call upon Him while He is near. Let the wicked forsake his way, and the unrighteous man his thoughts; let him return to the Lord, and He will have mercy on him; and to our God, for He will abundantly pardon. (Isaiah 55:6, 7)

And why would God want to be found? Because He's a God of relationships. This is one of the things that really sets Him apart from the pantheon of other gods that have been worshiped by human beings over the centuries.

Other gods were dictators. This may be one of the reasons we have trouble shaking that sort picture of God out of our minds. As the Christian church entered the Constantinian period, when Christianity became the official religion of the Roman Empire, numerous pagan concepts, traditions, and practices were adopted into the Christian church. A lot of people—especially those who joined the "new" religion for the sake of convenience or social acceptability—never really made a clean break with the gods of the Romans, Greeks or Barbarians.

The God of the Bible is different. He is a God of relationships. He didn't create us as slaves, but as companions. It's a point that shouldn't be missed. The government of God is not "top down" in the same sense as the absolute hierarchy of the Roman pantheon. Human beings were portrayed by the ancient pagan religions as the playthings of the gods; even though the God of the Bible is clearly on the throne of the universe in the Bible, He still calls human beings His *friends*:

And the Scripture was fulfilled which says, "Abraham believed God, and it was accounted to him for righteousness." And he was called the friend of God. (James 2:23)

And someone will say to him, "What are these wounds in your hands?" Then he will answer, "Those with which I was wounded in the house of my friends." (Zechariah 13:6)

No longer do I call you servants, for a servant does not know what his master is doing; but I have called you friends, for all things that I heard from My Father I have made known to you. (John 15:15)

What is my point? It's very simple. Those who expect God to demonstrate His reality through displays of power really don't understand the terms on which God Himself wants to relate to us. They're asking God to think and act like a human being, and, of course, that leads to disappointment. God reveals Himself—on His terms and in His way. It's not that we can't elicit a response from God, or that God isn't interested in answering prayer. Those who have carefully studied the principles of a solid prayer life and have learned to apply them repeatedly report dramatic answers to their prayers. If the primary subject of this book were prayer, I could list quite a number of dramatic answers I've received myself.

But for the purpose of answering the argument that God does not exist because demands on Him have gone unanswered, it's important to underline the fact that *real* prayer is something that occurs in the context of a relationship.

Miracles also occur in the context of a relationship. You'll notice that before the Red Sea was parted, Israel had to exercise faith in God's promise. They had to respond to His call, leave their homes in the land of Goshen, and follow Moses to the edge of the sea. And it wasn't until there were dust clouds on the horizon, kicked up by the pursuing armies of Pharaoh, that God parted the sea. Why? It's all about relationships. Trust. Commitment. God delights in working miracles, but He does it in the context of relationships. His delight is in working wonders for those who are sincerely interested in having Him as a part of their lives.

It's no accident that God uses the imagery of marriage to describe His relationship with His followers. (See, for example, the fifth chapter of Paul's letter to the Ephesians.) Young couples building a new relationship delight in pursuing each other and in *being* pursued. All cave man jokes aside, a young man doesn't really want to force a girl to marry him. Neither does a young lady really want to con a man into marrying her. Both of them want a relationship built on two-way trust. They have pursued each other and have been pursued *by* each other. The God who created us is like that. In fact, because we were created in His image, we can learn a lot about how God handles relationships from the way we wish our own relationships would play out.

If you want to understand why God doesn't simply part the clouds and make a public announcement to get everyone's attention, simply turn the relationship around in your mind for a moment. Try to put yourself in God's shoes. (I know it's impossible, but for the sake of the exercise, try it for a moment.) The God of the Bible is real. He's not a principle of physics or an unfeeling computer that runs the universe mechanically. He describes Himself as Someone with longings, desires, and emotions. And He delights in relationships. If you were longing for a good relationship with your creation, would you establish the relationship on the basis of the power you have over your creatures, or would you prefer relationships with people who *chose* you?

Any parent should understand this preference of God (not only does God compare His dealings with us to a marriage, He also uses the parent/child theme to make important points). If I want a relationship with my two daughters, I have a choice. I can wave around the wooden spoon (a favorite "tune-up" tool when I was growing up) and tell them to come to Daddy "or else." Even though I know I'm going to get compliance, it seems a little bit empty. I much prefer those moments when my little girl comes to me *voluntarily,* puts her arms around my neck and whispers, "Daddy, I love you!" Every parent knows what they'd prefer. God is no different with His children.

The Big Problem in the Universe

I know that this may not be enough for some people, so let's address another key reason why God doesn't always interfere in everyday life. It's found in the ancient book of Job, a book that many scholars feel might be the earliest contribution to the Bible. As the story opens, there's a council in heaven where "the sons of God came to present themselves before the Lord." (Job 1:6) And in the crowd, surprisingly, Satan appears. Why?

Some Bible students have concluded that since Adam is called the "son of God" (Luke 3:8) and because through sin Adam had surrendered dominion over the planet to Lucifer, the devil now appears in the heavenly council as a representative of the planet. He believes himself to be the rightful owner—a fact that is substantiated by his later offer to surrender the world to Jesus in exchange for worship.

Here's the interesting part of the story. God asks Lucifer where he's been, and the devil answers like this:

So Satan answered the Lord and said, "From going to and fro on the earth, and from walking back and forth on it." (Job 1:7b)

In the ancient world, walking over something was a symbol of ownership. When you laid your foot on a piece of real estate in a purposeful way, you were laying claim to that land as your own. In essence, the devil is claiming planet Earth as his own. When the human race fell into rebellion, they became enslaved and surrendered control of the planet to Lucifer.

So here's the big question: how is this possible? God has essentially allowed the devil enough leash to hang himself. Lucifer seized the planet and God has permitted the devil to operate for a time (the book of Revelation reveals that the devil knows his time is running out quickly). And God has chosen *not* to always interfere so that evil will play itself out publicly before the universe. That way, by showing the horrors of evil, He can put a permanent stop to it one day without having to cancel our gift of free will, while at the same time ensuring that the problem never comes up again. In order for us to learn to hate the rebellion we got ourselves into, He has to let us taste its consequences just long enough to make certain that it will never happen again.

Why doesn't God always show Himself?

1. He loves to be sought and found, like anyone else in a relationship. He doesn't jump to attention when we tell Him to.

2. He has a situation of rebellion on His hands that He needs to solve without violating our free will.

He really *has* shown Himself. In fact, there's abundant evidence all around us already. Sometimes we simply choose not to see it, just like the Pharisees of old. Part of the evidence is found in the scriptures, which are God's personal revelation to the human race. More evidence—powerful evidence—can be found in *another* book God speaks through quite loudly. We'll come back to this as our exploration continues.

CHAPTER FOUR

Arguments Against the Existence of God

Number Two: The Way So Many Christians Behave

One of the most common arguments against the existence of God is based on the behavior of those who claim to follow Him. The most common examples cited, understandably, are the Crusades and the Inquisition.

A typical argument would run something like this one I found on an atheist's website:

Is Christianity necessary for morality? Again all we have to do is look to history to see how Christians who believed in Jesus, God, and the Bible have behaved. Christianity introduced the Dark Ages, the Crusades, the Inquisition, and the witch burnings. Some of the most unspeakable evils have been committed in the name of God and religion. How is this possible if Christianity is supposed to be a religion of love? Christians insist that these things weren't done by "real" Christians. That is dishonest. The people who did them believed in Jesus. They believed in God. And they believed in the Bible. If they weren't "real" Christians, then when did the "real" Christian suddenly appear in history?[11]

At first blush, the argument seems pretty good—after all, who can deny that the organized Christian church has done some horrible things throughout the ages?

In a world used to skepticism, the Christian church can no longer stick its head in the sand about the atrocities committed in the name of Christ over the last two thousand years. This seems like a pretty good point.

But again, like many atheist arguments, it's based on a superficial understanding of Christianity. Is Christianity a religion of love? Absolutely. Even a cursory reading of the book of first John makes this abundantly clear:

35

He who says he is in the light, and hates his brother, is in darkness until now. He who loves his brother abides in the light, and there is no cause for stumbling in him. But he who hates his brother is in darkness and walks in darkness, and does not know where he is going, because the darkness has blinded his eyes. (1 John 2:9-11)

In this the children of God and the children of the devil are manifest: Whoever does not practice righteousness is not of God, nor is he who does not love his brother. (1 John 3:10)

Beloved, let us love one another, for love is of God; and everyone who loves is born of God and knows God. He who does not love does not know God, for God is love. (1 John 4:7, 8)

I could easily provide scores of examples from the Bible that clearly teach that Christians are supposed to *love*. In light of these texts, the atheists are right to point out that there seems to be a massive contradiction in the historical practice of Christianity. They believe the Christian religion to be a farce because so many Christians do not live up to the standards outlined in the Bible.

But there's a point in these verses that shouldn't be missed: why would John spend so much time teaching believers to discern between those whose have genuine faith and those who do not? The answer is simple: the problem of insincere Christians is as old as the religion itself. John is giving the early church a set of tools by which they can figure out who's for real and who isn't. In fact, much of the New Testament writings are dedicated to the subject of false Christianity.

When atheists scoff at the claim that those who did such horrible things during the Inquisition or the Crusades were not "real" Christians, they really miss the point. They seem to think that the Bible teaches that all will be well with the Christian church, and that our behavior proves the Bible false. But nothing could be further from the truth. In fact, the terrible atrocities committed in the name of Christ over the centuries only serve to *confirm* the Bible record.

Jesus Himself predicted that the Christian church would be a mix of genuine and superficial believers. His parable in the thirteenth chapter of Matthew should probably serve as our first example of Jesus' teaching on this subject:

Another parable He put forth to them, saying: "The kingdom of heaven is like a man who sowed good seed in his field; but while men slept, his enemy came and sowed tares among the wheat and went his way. But when the grain had sprouted and produced a crop, then the tares also appeared. So the servants of the owner came and said to him, 'Sir, did you not sow good seed in your field? How then does it have tares?' He said to them, 'An enemy has done this.' The servants said to him, 'Do you want us then to go and gather them up?' But he said, 'No, lest while you gather up the tares you also uproot the wheat with them. Let both grow together until the harvest, and at the time of harvest I will say to the reapers, "First gather together the tares and bind them in bundles to burn them, but gather the wheat into my barn."''' (Matthew 13:24-30)

Beginning in verse 37, Jesus explains the parable in detail. He is speaking primarily about the entire world rather than the church itself, but the point He makes is important. We need to be careful that we don't go about rooting out "evil" people, because in the process, we're likely to root out the good ones. And that's because we do not have the mind of God and are not capable of reading the human heart.

When Christians launched pogroms against non-Christians and "heretics" during the Dark Ages, they did so in *direct opposition* to the teachings of Jesus Christ. In this sense it is perfectly fair to describe the perpetrators as not being "real" Christians. It is in no sense dishonest, as the atheist website suggested, because the people who did such things were not following in the footsteps of Christ Himself—a fact the Bible itself points out in 1 John 2:6: "He who says he abides in Him ought himself also to walk just as He walked." If you want to assess Christianity itself, you need to start with its founder, not with those who lay claim to the title of "Christian." Would Jesus have slaughtered 50 million people (by some counts a conservative estimate) for matters of conscience? Absolutely not.

This is not, by any means, to suggest that we shouldn't also examine those who claim to follow Christ. On the contrary, the Bible is replete with warnings that we need to carefully judge the characters of those who present themselves as Christians to determine whether or not they are genuine. In fact, the Bible suggests that we need to start with *ourselves* in this process:

Examine yourselves as to whether you are in the faith. Test yourselves. Do you not know yourselves, that Jesus Christ is in you?—unless indeed you are disqualified. (2 Corinthians 13:5)

Is it possible to profess to be a Christian, even *believe* you are a Christian, and not really be one? According to the doctrines of atheism, no. According to the teachings of Christianity itself, yes! The words of Jesus found in the Sermon on the Mount sum it up nicely:

"Not everyone who says to Me, 'Lord, Lord,' shall enter the kingdom of heaven, but he who does the will of My Father in heaven. Many will say to Me in that day, 'Lord, Lord, have we not prophesied in Your name, cast out demons in Your name, and done many wonders in Your name?' And then I will declare to them, 'I never knew you; depart from Me, you who practice lawlessness!'" (Matthew 7:21-23)

To suggest that those who commit crimes in the name of Jesus "believed in Jesus and the Bible" is not a fair assessment. They may have professed Christianity, but they followed a Jesus they had reinvented to suit their own needs and/or philosophy.

The crimes of the Dark Ages were so horrendous (as are many of the atrocities committed in the name of Christ today) that it's easy to lose sight of the fact that not everyone was committing them. Many of the *victims* of the Inquisition, for example, were peaceable, sincere Christians. The victims tended to be religious people (there weren't many atheists) whose perspective on the faith differed greatly with those who ran the globally organized church of the day.

And that fact is perhaps one of the most stunning defenses of the authority of the Bible. Surprised? Many people are. The Bible *predicted* that there would be a massive problem inside Christianity. The fact that there has been such a large degree of deviation from the teachings of Christ among Christians does not prove the Bible false; on the contrary, it proves it to be true.

Follow the logic of the Apostle Paul very carefully as he writes to the Thessalonian church for the second time. They had been expecting the immediate return of Christ, within their lifetime, and Paul writes to correct their thinking:

Let no one deceive you by any means; for that Day will not come unless the falling away comes first, and the man of sin is revealed, the son of perdition, who opposes and exalts himself above all that is called God or that is worshiped, so that he sits as God in the temple of God, showing himself that he is God. (2 Thessalonians 2:3, 4)

Paul couldn't be clearer. Before Jesus returns there will be a great "falling away" and someone will try to pass himself off as God. This isn't talking about atheists, or communists, or even Satanists. It's talking about *Christians*.

Far from being caught off guard by the atrocities of the Dark Ages, the Bible *predicted* it.

One of the key problems that atheists often point to as a blight on the face of the Earth is the marriage between church and state. More than once I have seen notable atheists complain that religious people have all the power in this world, and they also have the habit of forcing everyone else to conform to their wishes. This, they argue, was one of the key problems that led to the cruelty of medieval Christianity and the harshness of life in countries governed by Islamic law—and they're absolutely right. The marriage of religion with civil government has almost always proved disastrous for the cause of human rights (outside of the theocracy of Israel)—a point I am willing to concede to the atheists.

The problem with this point as an argument against the authenticity of the Bible or the existence of God, however, is that, once again, the Bible clearly anticipates such developments. Carefully consider the following passage from the book of Revelation, written by a man who was condemned to exile by the Roman Empire because of his religious convictions:[12]

Then I stood on the sand of the sea. And I saw a beast rising up out of the sea, having seven heads and ten horns, and on his horns ten crowns, and on his heads a blasphemous name. Now the beast which I saw was like a leopard, his feet were like the feet of a bear, and his mouth like the mouth of a lion. The dragon gave him his power, his throne, and great authority. And I saw one of his heads as if it had been mortally wounded, and his deadly wound was healed. And all the world marveled and followed the beast. So they worshiped the dragon who gave authority to the beast; and they worshiped the beast, saying, "Who is like the beast? Who is able to make war with him?" And he was given a mouth speaking great things and blasphemies, and he was given authority to continue for forty-two months. Then he opened his mouth in blasphemy against God, to blaspheme His name, His tabernacle, and those who dwell in heaven. It was granted to him to make war with the saints and to overcome them. And authority was given him over every tribe, tongue, and nation. All who dwell on the earth will worship him, whose names have not been written in the Book of Life of the Lamb slain from the foundation of the world. (Revelation 13:1-8)

It would be easy to spend a couple of chapters on the thirteenth chapter of Revelation, but for the purposes of our present discussion let's touch on some of the highlights. The Bible anticipates a persecuting power that is both *religious* and *political.* Pay careful attention to the details:

• The beast from the sea is a composite animal made up of parts from a lion, bear, leopard, and horned beast. These animals are also mentioned in Daniel chapter seven, and have long been understood by Bible scholars to represent the kingdoms of Babylon, Medo-Persia, Greece, and Rome. They represent *political powers.*

• There are *crowns* on the *horns* of the beast, giving a two-fold indication that this is talking about a political institution. *Horns* were used in apocalyptic writings to represent political powers (see, for example, the parallel passage in Daniel 7:24); the symbolism of *crowns* should be obvious.

• This political power engages in blatantly religious activities: blaspheming God, persecuting God's people, and attempting to secure worship for itself.

Sometimes, when atheists complain about the hazards that can occur when the lines between church and state become a little too blurred, they seem to think that the Bible *teaches* Christians to seize the reigns of power and force their beliefs down the throats of their neighbors. There is certainly no question that this attitude rears its head within the broader community of Christianity from time to time. But to suggest that such behavior defines the essence of Christianity is dishonest. The Bible itself predicts such behavior and condemns it in the strongest language possible.

I strongly suspect that when skeptics denounce the teachings of the Bible because of the behavior of believers (and to condemn such behavior is laudable), they haven't really examined the teachings of the Bible carefully. Some people approach scripture as if it is a work of propaganda stitched together by people who need to defend their way of life—namely, Jews and Christians.

As a work of national or organizational propaganda, however, the Bible fails miserably: much of the Bible is dedicated to pointing out the character flaws of people who profess to follow God. Without batting an eyelash, the scriptures openly admit that Noah, a man who found favor in God's eyes, got foolishly drunk. It confesses that Abraham, the great father of the Hebrews, lied and risked his wife's purity and safety to save his own skin. It tells us that Moses, God's mouthpiece to the Israelites, lost his temper and murdered someone. David committed adultery and then killed his lover's husband. Peter denied Jesus publicly, and exhibited two different sets of behavior—one for Jews, and another for Gentiles. Judas, one of Jesus' own disciples, sold Him for thirty pieces of silver. Paul continued to struggle with sinful tendencies after his conversion. Ananias and Sapphira were liars. The list goes on and on.

The Bible as propaganda for God's people? Hardly. Most of what Paul wrote is actually devoted to condemning serious problems in the early Christian church. The Bible admits to shortcomings and serious errors in believers' lives. In fact, it comes down harder on God's people than on others.[13]

To suggest that the Bible paints a pretty picture of Christians is to admit that you haven't read it very carefully. Dwelling on the poor behavior of nominal Christians is a bit of a red herring. It distracts us from the real issue.

A while ago, a friend of mine told me the story of a man who found a card trick posted on a website. It showed him four ordinary playing cards and asked him to choose one of them *in his mind.* He wasn't to touch the computer or click on the card, just focus on one card and think about it. Once he picked his card, he clicked a button, and all four cards disappeared, and a moment later, three of them reappeared; every time he did it, it was *always* the three he didn't pick.

He was utterly baffled. How in the world could his computer know what he was thinking? Impossible! He went downstairs to tell his friend what he had discovered, and his friend said, "You mean you don't know how that's done? When you click the button, all the cards disappear, and *three completely different cards appear.* You're so busy concentrating on the one card that you don't pay careful attention to the other three, so when *they* don't reappear, you don't notice it!"

Do Christians misbehave? No question. No excuses. Supposed Christians have done—and continue to do—horrible things in the name of their religion. But it's entirely possible to focus so strongly on the negative behavior of Christians that you don't notice the obvious: there's horrible behavior *everywhere.* It's not a *Christian* trait; it's a *human* trait.

Richard Dawkins, in his book *The God Delusion,* seems to feel that immoral behavior is primarily a religious problem. After trying to explain away the atrocities of Stalin and Hitler, he goes so far as to make this statement:

Religious wars really are fought in the name of religion, and they have been horribly frequent in history. I cannot think of any war that has been fought in the name of atheism. Why should it? A war might be motivated by economic greed, by political ambition, by ethnic or racial prejudice, by deep grievance or revenge, or by patriotic belief in the destiny of a nation. [14]

Wars are not fought in the name of atheism? Let's unpack that statement a little bit. Dawkins is suggesting that atheists might start a war out of greed, political ambition, or racial prejudice; but never *because* they are atheists. (I should probably point out that the same benefit of the doubt is not extended to Christians.) This is hard to reconcile with the facts.

As I write, the Chinese government, founded on the principles of communism, is waging a war against religious people within their borders. Granted, they have not crossed international boundaries to engage the "enemy," but that does not make it any less an organized effort to fight philosophies that are viewed as being in competition with the ideology of the state. From the bulldozing of "unauthorized" Christian churches to the systematic persecution of practitioners of Falun Gong, the Chinese government has been waging war on religious believers of many faiths for years.

It might be argued by some that these pogroms are the result of the Chinese government's fear that popular religious movements would destabilize the country and rob the government of its power, and as such it is not really a war waged by "official atheism." But the question should be asked: if it's not an atheistic worldview at the base of communism, what is it?

Christians need to be honest and own up to their shortcomings. But atheists owe us the same courtesy. To suggest that the war on religion fought in communist countries isn't driven by an atheistic worldview simply isn't true; just ask the Christians who lived through it. Consider the account written by famous Soviet defector, Sergei Kourdadov, describing his assignment to a special police force designed to deal with thugs and the like. One day, his unit received special orders from a Communist Party official:

He went on, "I want you fellows to get some experience in the job before giving you the really important assignments. In the Soviet Union we have many types of criminals. We have antistate people who are murderers, drunkards, and prostitutes. You've been dealing with that kind. But they are really nothing.

"There are criminals who are a far greater threat to our country's security and our way of life. They are more dangerous because they work quietly in our midst, undermining the foundations of our system and threatening the existence of our country. The people I'm talking about look innocent on the outside. But don't be deceived. They spread their poisonous beliefs, threatening the life of our society, poisoning our children's minds with false teachings, and undermining the doctrines of Leninism and Marxism. These are the religiozniki, the religious Believers."

I didn't catch what he said at first. But he repeated it. "It's the religozniki." He wanted to make sure we all got what he was saying.

"These are the Believers," he continued, "who have organized an active program which threatens the great accomplishments of the Soviet people. They actively aid the enemies of our country. They go hand in hand with the imperialists and attempt to overthrow or set back the achievements of the Communist party of the Soviet Union." By now he had become greatly impassioned. We could tell how deeply he felt about what he was saying. "They are even more dangerous because they do not appear to be dangerous. Murderers and thieves are direct. These people are deceptive and cunning and clever. Before you know it, they have undermined the things we've worked so hard for, poisoned the people, and done their damage."

"Now, that's why you've been selected as a special police-operations squad—to be an action group against the enemies. You've been given practical experience; now it's time for your real work. Your unit is one of many that are being established throughout our country. It's time we put a stop to these enemies.

"We must take direct action! That's your job. The orders for your operations come directly from the party bureau and Comrade Brezhnev. From Moscow your orders come directly to Gorkom here, and we pass them along to Comrade Nikiforov, who will be your immediate superior...." [15]

It's far too convenient to describe these sorts of accounts as purely political. Atheists don't get to wash their hands of this problem quite so easily. Prominent skeptics like Mr. Dawkins like to suggest that people like Stalin were not *influenced* to evil by their atheistic philosophy, but it's pretty hard to separate someone's worldview from their behavior. I will entirely concede the point that Stalin behaved differently as an atheist than most other atheists would. I will also concede the point that Stalin obviously didn't understand an atheistic worldview like most modern atheists would, and that Mr. Dawkins himself would never be driven to behave like Stalin by *his* atheism. But why are atheists so hesitant to make the same concession for Christians—to admit that those who are driven by religious fervor to commit atrocities might be operating in contradiction to the way most practicing Christians would understand the Christian religion?

Again, I must underline an important point. When someone kills in the name of Christ, he is in direct violation of the teachings of Christ. I can open my Bible and show you where it tells us not to do such things. That can't be easily done with atheists who commit atrocities, because there is no such thing as a *right* or *wrong* perspective on atheism. When Stalin murders millions as an atheist, what evidence can the atheist provide that Stalin did something *wrong* other than his or her own point of view?

We should also probably flip the coin and ask another good question. Instead of focusing only on evil, let's look at the good done by professing Christians. If atheism is a morally superior system of belief, as suggested by so many atheistic apologists, we should find not only less evil, but also more good. Where are the atheist hospitals? Where are the organized atheistic relief workers? They're not easy to find.

Here's the long and the short of this chapter: the problem of evil is not a *religious* problem; it's a *human* problem. The existence of poor behavior among God's people is not proof that God doesn't exist; it only underlines what God has said all along:

"The heart is deceitful above all things, and desperately wicked; who can know it? I, the Lord, search the heart, I test the mind, even to give every man according to his ways, according to the fruit of his doings."
(Jeremiah 17:9, 10)

It would seem that the world is pretty much the way God described it.

CHAPTER FIVE

The Fruits of Atheism

*How the theory of evolution has
fueled its share of human suffering and even helped
fuel one of the worst wars in history.*

There are few people who are not amazed at the miracle of human birth, evolutionists included. (In fact, many prominent defenders of Darwinian evolution enthusiastically state their sense of wonder at the discoveries they make in the natural world.) In the space of nine short months, a single cell with a complete set of blueprints for life divides millions of times until it becomes a seven or eight-pound bundle of joy.

Modern technology has given us the privilege of peeking inside the womb during gestation so that we can actually *watch* the various stages of prenatal development take place.

We don't all see the same thing when we peek inside the womb, however. Some people are awestruck because they see a human being developing in the image of the Creator. But others see something completely different: a scaled-down reenactment of the evolutionary process.

The theory, in its original form, runs something like this: the human fetus starts out as a single-celled organism, because our most distant ancestors were supposedly single-celled beings. The fetus is therefore believed to be reliving our existence as it was billions of years ago. Then, on about the eighth day of pregnancy, the single cell becomes a *blastula*, a structure of cells that resembles a hollow sphere. It is said that the fetus now resembles ancient sea sponges, another supposed evolutionary ancestor.

After thirty days, the fetus is thought to pass into a stage that resembles a fish, which supposedly came into existence about half a billion years ago, and advocates of the theory of recapitulation are quick to point out little folds in the fetus' neck that resemble gill slits. After the fetus passes through the fish stage of its existence, it moves on to a lizard stage, an observation stemming in part from the appearance of a "tail." After the lizard stage, the fetus begins to resemble a primate, covered with fine hair and still hanging on to the remnants of what looks like a tail. Finally, after about two months of development, the baby begins to look human.

Famous baby expert, Dr. Benjamin Spock, summarized the theory like this:

Each child as he develops is retracing the whole history of mankind, physically and spiritually, step by step. A baby starts off in the womb as a single tiny cell, just the way the first living thing appeared in the ocean. Weeks later, as he lies in the amniotic fluid of the womb, he has gills like a fish...[16]

This theory is known by a number of different names: the biogenetic law, Haeckel's law, the theory of recapitulation, and the impressive sounding phrase, "ontogeny recapitulates phylogeny." It was first popularized in 1866 by the zoologist Ernst Haeckel, and somewhat like the process of evolution, the theory itself has changed with the passage of time. The core concept, however, remains intact.[17]

Haeckel was born in 1834 in the city of Potsdam. He received his medical degree from the University of Berlin in 1857, and went on to teach comparative anatomy at the University of Jena. It was at Jena that he became the first person to promote Darwinism in the German language.

He believed there must be some unifying principle that would unite the various disciplines that interested him: things like the sciences, philosophy, and religion. The theory of evolution struck him as the answer, and building on Darwin, he published his "theory of recapitulation."

It turns out that Mr. Haeckel's skill set spilled over into areas beyond science. He was a pretty good artist, too. He made sketches of human, monkey and dog fetuses, and then put them side by side to make comparisons. He did the same thing with pigs, bulls, and rabbits. His sketches were made into woodcut drawings and published.

Haeckel's drawings were very convincing and easy to study, because each of them was blown up to about one hundred times the size of an actual fetus. It was difficult to tell the difference between human and animal fetuses, and Haeckel explained that the reason was because in the earliest stages of development, all living creatures are virtually the same.

His argument was convincing, and it caught on like wildfire. Before long, the better part of the German scientific community was endorsing it as proof of our development from lower forms of life. And although modern biology rejects much of the theory today, it can still be found in school textbooks.

There is no question that the theory seemed brilliant. There was just one small problem: his drawings were fraudulent. He purposely manipulated the drawings to make the fetuses look alike:

The idea is now known to be completely false. It is therefore not surprising that Haeckel could not find sufficient anatomical evidence to make his theory convincing. Never one to let lack of evidence stand in his way, Haeckel manufactured the "evidence" by fraudulently changing the drawings of embryos by two other scientists.

In his book Natürliche Schöpfungs-geschichte (The Natural History of Creation), published in German in 1868 (and in English in 1876 with the title The History of Creation), Haeckel used the drawing of a 25-day-old dog embryo which had been published by T.L.W. Bischoff in 1845, and that of a 4-week-old human embryo published by A. Ecker in 1851. Wilhelm His, Sr (1831-1904), a famous comparative embryologist of the day and professor of anatomy at the University of Leipzig, uncovered the fraud.

Prof. His showed in 1874 that Haeckel had added 3.5 mm to the head of Bischoff's dog embryo, taken 2 mm off the head of Ecker's human embryo, doubled the length of the human posterior, and substantially altered the details of the human eye. He sarcastically pointed out that Haeckel taught in Jena, home of the then finest optical equipment available, and so had no excuse for inaccuracy. He concluded that anyone who engaged in such blatant fraud had forfeited all respect and that Haeckel had eliminated himself from the ranks of scientific research workers of any stature.[18]

Haeckel later admitted to playing loose with the facts, stating that he had taken the liberty of filling in where facts seemed to be missing. When his dishonesty was discovered, he was called to appear before the university court where five of his colleagues charged him with fraud. His forgeries were then made public in the book *Haeckel's Frauds and Forgeries*, published in 1911.

Today most scientists admit that Haeckel was wrong. Some have pointed out that the fetuses portrayed in the illustrations look similar only at a particular stage of development, but are quite dissimilar earlier on—a fact that would have immediately discredited the theory. But in spite of the fraudulent nature of Haeckel's work, the theory hasn't been easy to weed out of human thinking. Back in 1969 Walter Bock made an important observation in the magazine *Science*:

. . . the biogenetic law has become so deeply rooted in biological thought that it cannot be weeded out in spite of its having been demonstrated to be wrong by numerous subsequent scholars. Even today both subtle and overt uses of the biogenetic law are frequently encountered in the general biological literature as well as in more specialized evolutionary and systematic studies.[19]

You would think that in the decades since Mr. Bock wrote these words the theory would have been completely uprooted from the textbooks of the civilized world, but sadly, the theory continues to survive in classrooms in one form or another. Essentially, we continue to perpetuate a fraud.

If the theory *were* true, you'd expect bird embryos to have fish-like characteristics and monkey embryos to have bird-like characteristics, because so-called higher life forms would have inherited traits from their ancestors. But you certainly wouldn't expect to find bird-like characteristics in a fish or monkey-like characteristics in a bird, because birds supposedly appeared on Earth after fish, and primates are supposedly more advanced life forms than birds. And yet bird embryos appear to have a monkey-like tail, and fish embryos appear to have a bird-like yolk sac. Quite contrary to Haeckel's suggestion, physiological similarities do not require that one animal be a descendant of the other.

To be fair, most evolutionists have a more sophisticated theory than simple descendancy. It is not assumed, for example, that modern birds descended from modern lizards, but rather that their common features indicate a shared ancestry. The word *homogeny* is used by biologists to describe physiological similarities between different species.

The bones in a whale's flipper, for example, bear a striking resemblance to the bones in the human hand, and it is suggested that the reason for this is that mammals share common ancestors in the evolutionary tree. However, this is no means the only explanation for the similarities: it is also possible that all living creatures had a common Designer.

Just as houses designed by one architect have many similar features, and experts in architecture can often guess who designed a building based on those features, we should expect that if life on Earth had a common Architect, we would find similarities of design.

I suppose one of the best questions we could ask at this point is: *so what?* What harm is Haeckel's silly little theory? The answer? It helped to fuel one of the worst wars in human history.

Let's go back and examine carefully the world into which Haeckel brought his theory. In Germany, there was a romantic revival of Teutonic mythology taking place, which popularized the idea that the Germanic peoples were descendants of an ancient race known as the Aryans. As a result of this heritage, they were considered superior to the other races around them. Not only was the idea found in popular articles and magazines, it actually made its way into the university classrooms well in advance of the Nazis' rise to power. German nationalism was also on the rise, spurred along by the idea that the Aryan bloodline was in danger of being watered down. Some began to dream of a new German belief system, divorced from Christianity and based on ancient German folklore, that would unite the nation.

Ernst Haeckel was a vocal proponent of this new wave of nationalism, and he found in Darwinism the philosophical glue he believed would hold together the new German society. He falsified the results of his studies to make his point: the Germans are, indeed, a superior people. How did his theory accomplish this?

Haeckel influenced a *lot* of people. After he originally published his theory in 1866, others, driven by the racist spirit of the age, took his theory further. If the human fetus passes through several *animal* stages of development in the womb, perhaps in the last part of gestation it also passes through several human stages of evolutionary development as well, from the earliest primitive human up through the most advanced versions of *Homo sapiens.*

This understanding of embryonic development, of course, played right into the hands of the "Volkish" movement that was growing in Germany. Scholars (yes, *scholars*) began to look at other races and explain their physiological differences as the product of varying degrees of evolutionary development. Some races were believed to be more ancient than others, and thus more primitive (a theory that has not yet entirely evaporated from some peoples' minds). The so-called "inferior" races were said to be in earlier stages of evolutionary development, which in turn engendered a great deal of pride among those who believed themselves to be more advanced.

In fact, in 1866, the same year that Haeckel published his biogenetic law, Dr. John Down of England described a mental condition we know today as "Down syndrome," caused by the presence of a 47th chromosome. Dr. Down didn't know the genetic cause of the condition, of course; he simply referred to it as *Mongoloid Idiocy*. (The unfortunate label "mongoloid" stubbornly persisted until only very recently.) What few people realize is the reason Down syndrome victims were once called "mongoloids" is because it was believed they were stuck in a more primitive stage of human evolution.

Thanks to Darwinism, people in Dr. Down's day believed that the Mongoloid race was less evolved than the Caucasian race. When something went wrong with a baby's prenatal development, it was believed that it was sometimes the result of incomplete recapitulation. The baby had failed to pass through all the previous stages of evolution, and although it may be part of the Caucasian race, it came out of the womb having one or two features that looked more Mongoloid than Caucasian.

Naturally, we recoil at such ideas, but it goes to prove how widespread Mr. Haeckel's type of thinking was. It gave birth to a whole new variety of racism. And it must be pointed out that this was not empirical science; it was a deliberate attempt to infuse the practice of science with racist ideology.

Far from being benign, the philosophy of atheism has made major contributions to human suffering and injustice. Robert Lifton, in his book *The Nazi Doctor: Medical Killing and the Psychology of Genocide*, makes this interesting observation:

Haeckel embraced a widely held nineteenth-century theme.... that each of the major races of humanity can be considered a separate species. Haeckel believed that varied races of mankind are endowed with differing hereditary characteristics not only of color but, more important, of intelligence, and that external physical characteristics are a sign of innate and moral capacity.... Haeckel went so far as to say, concerning these 'lower races' ('wooly-haired' Negroes), that since they are 'psychologically nearer to the mammals (apes and dogs) than to civilized Europeans, we must, therefore, assign a totally different value to their lives.[20]

How were otherwise rational Nazis able to bring themselves to conduct the wholesale slaughter of other people? They had learned to think of them as a *different species.* Doctors sworn to uphold life, for example, came to the misguided conclusion that to obliterate lower life forms was to preserve and advance the health of the master race. One writer puts it like this:

For Nazi doctors initially trained in the healing arts to be cool, detached practitioners of euthanasia—"direct medical killing"—and directing the "killing program" at Auschwitz "from beginning to end," the boundary between healing and killing had to be destroyed. The scientific tradition established by the work of Haeckel and his followers enabled the Nazi doctors to erase the healing/killing boundary by enforcing the grandiose Volkish mission for the healing of the German race by killing off the "lower races." It was the stamp of scientific legitimacy afforded by academia that enabled the great evils to come.[21]

While the revival of Germanic mythology certainly had something to do with a growing anti-Semitism in Germany, we should be clear that Darwinism played more than a supporting role. As people shook off the notion of a Creator God, they began to view human beings as nothing more than part of the animal kingdom. Suddenly finding themselves without a clearly defined morality for human civilization in the absence of God, they had to turn to nature itself for guidelines. There they discovered a raw struggle for survival, and since human beings were no longer believed to be created above the animal kingdom, they reasoned that the same rules of "survival of the fittest" should apply to us. Killing off inferior races was just part of the process of evolution.

The implications for atheism and Darwinism are grave; so grave, in fact, that renowned atheist Richard Dawkins makes a heroic effort to distance Hitler from the theory of evolution in his 2006 book, *The God Delusion:*

The legend that Hitler was an atheist has been assiduously cultivated, so much so that a great many people believe it without question, and it is regularly and defiantly trotted out by religious apologists. The truth of the matter is far from clear. Hitler was born into a Catholic family, and went to Catholic schools and churches as a child. Obviously that is not significant in itself: he could easily have given it up, as Stalin gave up his Russian Orthodoxy after leaving the Tiflis Theological Seminary. But Hitler never formally renounced his Catholicism, and there are indications throughout his life that he remained religious.[22]

Let's push the pause button for a moment. Hitler *was* a Catholic Christian, back in 1914. Does the fact that he never publicly renounced his faith mean that he remained a Catholic all his life? In the New Testament accounts, Judas never publicly renounced Christ, and yet you could hardly argue that Judas was a true follower of Christ in the end.

You don't have to issue a public renunciation—print a retraction in the paper—in order to abandon your faith! Dawkins admits as much, and goes on to examine Hitler's later life for evidence that he was still operating as a Christian during the death-camp years. Dawkins points out, "as late as 1941 he told his adjutant, General Gerhard Engel, 'I shall remain a Catholic forever.'"[23]

I don't doubt for a moment that Hitler uttered those words. Does that make him a practicing Christian? Hardly. As a minister I have heard many people say that they will be "Christians forever," even when their lives tell a completely different story. All it means is that they are genuinely confused as to what it actually *means* to be a Christian. In Hitler's case, he could have meant a number of things by those words. He might have meant that he knew his name would remain on a church membership list the rest of his life. He may have been lamenting the fact that he had trouble completely abandoning some of the habits he had been raised with, which he attributed to Catholicism. But it is certainly not clear that Hitler murdered Jews *as a Catholic.*

Dawkins then ratchets up his argument by pointing out that Hitler was blaming the Jews for Germany's problems. Back in 1923 Hitler made a speech in Munich where he said, "The first thing to do is rescue [Germany] from the Jew who is ruining our country.... We want to prevent our Germany from suffering, as Another did, the death upon the Cross."[24]

I know this looks pretty bad for Christianity, but let's examine the facts. Did Hitler use Christian language as he built his perverted dream for Germany? Apparently so—at least on this occasion. But an allusion to the story of Christ's crucifixion in a speech is not the same thing as building a program of genocide on Christian theology. Hitler was simply using an analogy to make a point. That statement no more made him a practicing Christian than reference to Greek mythology in this book would make me a practicing Greek pagan.

Mr. Dawkins is trying to lay the blame for Hitler's philosophy at the feet of the Christians—a conclusion that is laden with problems. I won't deny that the organized Christian church has done awful things and has, on occasion, promoted terrible ideas. I'll be the first to admit that Rome turned a blind eye to much of what was going on in Germany during the Second World War. That much is a matter of public record. Have some Christians been anti-Semites? Yes. But to suggest that Hitler was operating his death camps because he was a *Christian* is ludicrous.

Not everybody on church rolls is actually a practicing Christian, and it has been well documented that the religious inspiration for the Nazi regime came primarily from the occult and pagan Germanic mythology.

To suggest that atheism or Darwinism had nothing to do with it is just as ludicrous. It was not the Bible that gave the operators of the death camps the rationale they needed to justify the mass execution of "inferior" races. The belief that some races were genetically inferior— maybe even a different species—didn't come from the Christian scriptures. (In fact, Paul is crystal clear in his statement in Acts 17 that "… He has made from one blood every nation of men to dwell on all the face of the earth….") Let's be honest about it: the Bible did not fuel those ideas; they were fueled by the apostles of Darwin, the sketches of Haeckel, and the writings of the atheist philosopher Nietzsche.

To be perfectly fair with Mr. Dawkins, I should probably point out that he concedes the point that Hitler may have given up his Christianity. He even provides the following 1941 Hitler quotations which seem to underscore the point:

The heaviest blow that ever struck humanity was the coming of Christianity. Bolshevism is Christianity's illegitimate child. Both are inventions of the Jew. The deliberate lie in the matter of religion was introduced into the world by Christianity….

The reason why the ancient world was so pure, light and serene was that it knew nothing of the two great scourges: the pox and Christianity.

When all is said, we have no reason to wish that the Italians and Spaniards should free themselves from the drug of Christianity. Let's be the only people who are immunised against the disease.[25]

My hat is off to Mr. Dawkins for being so honest as to provide these quotations. They come from the same year that Hitler is supposed to have confessed to Gerhard Engel that he would "remain a Catholic forever." It is obvious that, in reality, Hitler hated Christianity. Like many modern atheists, he considered it to be a blight on the world.

As a last ditch attempt to hang the blame for the death camps on religion, Richard Dawkins points out that Hitler continued to use religious language:

Even when he was railing against Christianity, Hitler never ceased using the language of Providence: a mysterious agency which, he believed, had singled him out for a divine mission to lead Germany. He sometimes called it Providence, at other times God. After the Anschluss, *when Hitler returned in triumph to Vienna in 1938, his exultant speech mentioned God in this providential guise: "I believe it was God's will to send a boy from here into the Reich, to let him grow up and to raise him to be the leader of the nation so that he could lead back his homeland into the Reich."* [26]

One huge problem immediately emerges from Dawkins' use of this kind of language to prove that Hitler was religious. At the beginning of the same book, Dawkins ridicules Christians who claim Einstein was religious because he invoked the name of God:

There is every reason to think that famous Einsteinisms like "god is subtle but he is not malicious" or "He does not play dice" or "Did god have a choice in creating the Universe?" are pantheistic, not deistic, and certainly not theistic. "God does not play dice" should be translated as "Randomness does not lie at the heart of all things." "Did God have a choice in creating the Universe?" means "Could the universe have begun in any other way?" Einstein was using 'God' in a purely metaphorical, poetic sense. So is Stephen Hawking, and so are most of those physicists who occasionally slip into the language of religious metaphor. [27]

It would seem a little inconsistent to allow this use of the word "God" for physicists, but question the same possibility for Hitler, whose actions and subsequent statements make it abundantly clear that he did not believe in the Christianity of the Bible. Trace the line of thought in pre-war Germany very carefully, and the ugly truth rises to the surface. Darwinism, taken to its logical conclusion, is capable of producing some horrific suffering.

Christians have, by and large, started to take ownership of the inexcusable anti-Semitism they have occasionally practiced in contradiction to the teachings of Christ over the centuries. They recognize it as being inconsistent with the teachings of their faith. Darwinists will ultimately have more trouble finding a way to condemn the death camps. To be sure, they *do* condemn them, but on what basis—the sanctity of human life? What exactly makes life sacred for the atheist? Is it our collective opinion? The vote of the majority? Without God in the picture, what is the objective standard of morality?

To be sure, evolutionists and atheist philosophers have attempted to make cases for a system morality without God, but ultimately, such systems will always be a matter of human opinion. If there is no God, who's to say I'd be wrong if I murdered my neighbor? Even if everyone in the world voted that I was wrong, that wouldn't necessarily make it so. It would still be their version of morality versus mine, without a higher court to decide the truth. Morality becomes a matter of majority opinion.

There have been occasions in human history where the majority has clearly been wrong. There were more Hutus in Rwanda than Tutsis (85 percent of the population) before the genocide, and the Hutus said the Tutsis should die. The Hutus had a rationale for their actions: they believed they were defending the survival of their own kind. In their way of thinking, eliminating the Tutsis made life better for the Hutus. It was survival of the fittest. What could possibly be more Darwinian than *that*?

I suppose you could conceivably argue that the act of genocide should be *ruled* to be immoral for the sake of everyone. If we're smart, after all, we'll recognize that we might one day be the minority that is persecuted, and to agree that genocide is morally wrong is in our own best interests. But a majority vote simply doesn't make things *wrong*. The majority of people agree that forbidding genocide is a good idea.

But what happens when attitudes shift and the majority begin to believe that genocide is the right thing to do? If the prohibition against genocide was originally only a humanly devised social contract, who's to say that the *new* contract is morally wrong? The majority that once proclaimed it *wrong* can just as easily change the ruling and decide that it's *right*.

Atheism is fraught with moral problems that are much more complicated than the atrocities committed by so-called Christians acting in direct contradiction to the tenets of their faith. Atheists have ridiculed belief on the basis of the actions of believers, and have gone as far as to suggest that *they* would never do such things. But this is not honest, and it's time that atheists and Darwinists owned up to their own contribution to human misery.

CHAPTER SIX

Arguments Against the Existence of God

Number Three: If God Exists, He Would Eliminate Suffering

A friend of mine approached me after church one day with tears in his eyes. "Pastor," he said, "I've got to talk to you."

We slipped into a side room to talk. I discovered that he had been attending a public university where some of the values he had grown up with were being challenged by skeptical professors.

"Tell me what's bothering you," I said.

A tear began to well up in the corner of his eye, and his voice began to shake. It took a moment for him to say something. "Pastor," he said, "some old used caskets have been found, with scratch marks on the *inside of the lid.* The people they buried weren't even dead! How in the world could God let something like that happen?"

He's not the first to ask such questions. Skeptics love to point to the existence of human suffering as evidence that God does not exist. Philosophers describe this as the "problem of evil." If God is all-powerful, all-knowing, and perfectly good, why in the world does He permit human suffering? Couldn't He simply eliminate it? The argument often runs something like this version I found posted on the Internet:

1. If God exists, then God is omnipotent, omniscient, and morally perfect.

2. If God is omnipotent, then God has the power to eliminate all evil.

3. If God is omniscient, then God knows when evil exists.

4. If God is morally perfect, then God has the desire to eliminate all evil.

5. Evil exists.

6. If evil exists and God exists, then either God doesn't have

the power to eliminate all evil, or doesn't know when evil
exists, or doesn't have the desire to eliminate all evil.
7. Therefore, God doesn't exist.

Before I address the argument itself, I should point out something
interesting. The fifth point states, "evil exists," which is a statement
that would be hard to make without the existence of God. Apart
from a definition provided by someone outside of ourselves, how do
we know what evil is? Do we define "evil" as those things that cause
discomfort or pain? Or perhaps an activity is "evil" when more people
suffer harm than derive benefit. Is "evil" simply that which makes us
unhappy?

Those sorts of definitions are immediately problematic. If evil is
simply that which causes discomfort or pain, then do we classify things
like chemotherapy or a root canal as evil? If we define an activity that
causes more harm to more people than it benefits, does that excuse
something like the 1994 Rwandan genocide, where a majority of
Hutus sought to improve their own lot by eliminating the minority
Tutsis? These are not good definitions of evil.

Darwinism leaves us with no objective definitions of good and evil.
They simply become social conventions or accidental byproducts of
the evolutionary process. We might collectively *feel* that something
is wrong, but apart from our feelings, there is simply no way to
objectively determine whether or not it really *is* wrong. The following
quotation, attributed to Richard Dawkins, sums up the position:

The universe we observe today has precisely the properties we should expect
if there is at the bottom no design, no purpose, no evil and no good, nothing
but pointless indifference.[28]

The ramifications of this statement are profound. It essentially
states that if human beings hadn't defined evil, it wouldn't exist. It
suggests that there really is no such thing as an objective standard
of right and wrong—a notion that has become popular in modern
university philosophy classes. We are simply left to define morality for
ourselves.

But we're a little off track now, so let's get back to the argument
itself. It essentially states that if God hates suffering, and He has the
power to do something about it, He would. Because we can see no
abatement of evil in this world, God must not exist.

As pointed out in an earlier chapter, we must be careful not to pretend that we can think like God. It may be true that if *we* were in charge of the universe for twenty-four hours, and given the gift of unlimited power, we would simply wipe out all suffering. But that's a little reminiscent of a five-year old who wants something *now* because he's unable to carefully weigh the long-term consequences of his decision. If I asked my four-year-old if she wants ten dollars now or a hundred dollars in a month, she'll likely pick the ten dollars. To the adult world, that seems like a foolish decision. When you're four, it makes perfect sense.

Could it be, when we're busy making proclamations about what God should do about the suffering in this world, that we're trying to grab ten dollars instead of waiting for a hundred? Our biggest problem as finite human beings is that we find it difficult to understand things that operate on a higher plane of existence than we do.

Fortunately, God chooses to reveal Himself to us, which is why Christians often refer to their system of belief as a "revealed" religion. With a little bit of careful study, it's amazing what God permits us to figure out.

One day, a kindergarten teacher gave her students a simple assignment: take some crayons and draw a picture. Most of the children did exactly what you'd expect them to do. They drew simple stick pictures of families, houses and animals. Most of them were done in about ten minutes. One little girl, however, kept working long after the other children were finished.

"What are you drawing?" the teacher asked.

"I'm drawing God," she said.

"But honey, nobody really knows what God looks like!"

The little girl lifted her green crayon off the page for a moment and thought about it very carefully. "Well," she said, "when I'm finished with this picture, they will!"

What *does* God look like? The world seems so black and white for children. Answers come easy. But when we grow up and have to face the ugly realities of life on planet Earth, we're not so quick to answer. We ask ourselves *why* God would allow these things to happen when He's supposed to be able to stop them. We're tempted to think that God either isn't powerful enough to do something, or that He just doesn't care.

Skeptics point to the problem and laugh. "See? There's no good explanation for that, so God must not exist at all."

There's only one problem with this argument: the Bible *does* explain it. It just requires a little careful homework. It takes sixty-six books for the writers of the Bible to present the problem and its solution. We can't expect to come up with it in five minutes any more than I could expect to earn a doctorate in nuclear physics in the course of a week.

The Bible gives reasonable answers to some of life's toughest questions. It pulls back the curtains of the universe and allows us to see what's going on behind the scenes:

And war broke out in heaven: Michael and his angels fought against the dragon; and the dragon and his angels fought, but they did not prevail, nor was a place found for them in heaven any longer. (Revelation 12:7, 8)

According to the Bible, the first place you find war in the universe is *not* between neighboring tribes of cavemen or on the battlefields of ancient civilizations. Surprisingly, the problem of war started in *heaven.* This shows us that God is not immune to suffering. He is not the God of the *deists,* who believe that He started the world spinning thousands of years ago and then went on a vacation.

God does not live in an isolation chamber where He doesn't have to deal with pain or suffering. Furthermore, He made a decision to *do* something about it:

So the great dragon was cast out, that serpent of old, called the Devil and Satan, who deceives the whole world; he was cast to the earth, and his angels were cast out with him. (Revelation 12:9)

I believe this is a literal account of something that really happened. Skeptics will have difficulty with this story because they do not believe in angels, demons, or God. They will want to understand this passage in allegorical terms, dismissing it as apocalyptic literature. The all-important point, however, is still there: the Bible recognizes the problem of evil. And it gives us enough information to help us think through the issue carefully.

When I was a kid, I wasn't happy with the explanation given in Revelation chapter twelve. That's all God did? Kick the devil out of heaven? What kind of solution is *that*? If *I* had been in charge, I would have wiped Lucifer out of existence on the spot! But let's think things through very carefully. Let's suppose you have twelve children, and one of them begins to challenge your authority in front of the others. To make matters worse, some of his siblings have been listening to his arguments and are starting to follow in his footsteps. What are you going to do?

Do you take your rebellious child out behind the house and have him shot? That kind of reaction might bring short-term relief, but in the long run it's going to cause some real problems. There's no question the surviving children will likely toe the line for a while, exhibiting model obedience; but their obedience has nothing to do with love and respect. They probably *hate* you at this point, but they're afraid of what you might do if they don't comply with your rules. You no longer have a home; you have a concentration camp.

Let's think about an ideal universe for a moment. The Bible defines God as "love." In order to love, you must be free to *choose*. If you can't make the choice to walk away from a relationship, it isn't very meaningful. This would hold true for both God and the people who enter into a relationship with Him.

The fact that my wife stays with me of her own free will is something that gives me joy every day of my life. Our relationship is real. She *chooses* to stay with me. If I had to chain her to a post to keep her around, I might still have a wife, but we'd have no relationship. Real love must be exercised in the context of the freedom of choice. Otherwise, all you have is a jailer/prisoner relationship instead of a meaningful personal relationship that results in joy.

God created us with the freedom to choose so that we could have a significant personal relationship with Him. We were created with the ability to rebel so that our choice to live in harmony with God would be meaningful. And the question that naturally arises out of that situation, of course, is *why*. Why would God take such a risk?

Ask any parent why they choose to have a baby when there are so many risks involved. Why have children when one of them might break your heart and go to jail? Why start a family when, in spite of your best efforts to build a good relationship, your child might choose to move away and break off all contact?

Why bring children into this world when they might choose to become a problem for the rest of society? The answer is simple: the value of a good personal relationship with your children is significant enough that it's worth the risk.

Tuck that thought behind one ear and go back to the Bible's record of what actually happened as one angel decided to exercise his freedom of choice and turn his back on God:

How you are fallen from heaven, O Lucifer, son of the morning! How you are cut down to the ground, you who weakened the nations! For you have said in your heart: "I will ascend into heaven, I will exalt my throne above the stars of God; I will also sit also upon the mount of the congregation on the farthest sides of the north; I will ascend above the heights of the clouds, I will be like the most High." (Isaiah 14:12-14)

One angel suddenly began to think he was better suited than God Himself to run the universe, so he launched a malicious campaign to seize the throne. It was the first coup attempt in history, fueled by a hateful propaganda campaign. A corrupted angel apparently started to spread lies about the nature and character of God, suggesting that something was wrong with His government. And it's at this point that God removes Lucifer from the kingdom of heaven.

It's important to understand that God didn't *create* a devil; He *discovered* one. I know that distinction won't make everybody happy, but it's an important one. In the book of Ezekiel, God underscores the fact that Lucifer was perfect until iniquity was *found* in him:

You were perfect in your ways from the day you were created, till iniquity was found in you. (Ezekiel 28:15)

The fallen angel had to go—which again raises the question: why not simply destroy him? Don't forget that if Lucifer had freedom of choice; so did every other angel. According to the twelfth chapter of Revelation, about one-third of them followed Lucifer into rebellion. His ideas had become widespread. If all of the rebels were suddenly wiped out of existence, what would the remaining angels think? *Maybe Lucifer was right! Maybe there is something wrong with God's government. After all, He destroyed Lucifer like He was afraid of something.*

It's easy for us to argue that God should wipe out all trace of evil from the face of the planet. But don't forget what that would cost: *everything* with a trace of evil in it (or the potential for it) would have to be eliminated. It wouldn't leave much behind. Nobody would survive. Not even you.

When skeptics charge God with wrongdoing because He's supposed to be a God of love, they haven't thought the issue through very carefully. A sudden expunging of evil from this planet would leave almost nothing behind, including the skeptics themselves. God would eliminate suffering, but lose something of infinite value: His creation. Sure, He could wipe it all out and start over with people who wouldn't cause pain, but those replacement people aren't *you*. It's not just *somebody* God wants in His life: it's *you*.

There's a reason children don't want a replacement dog when a car hits theirs: they want *their* dog. Parents don't simply shrug their shoulders when one of their children has terminal cancer because they can always have another baby. They want to save the child they love. And that's why God didn't simply wipe it out and start over. *We mean something to Him.*

God is walking a fine line of His own choosing. He must eliminate pain and suffering (the thing that skeptics demand of Him) without utterly destroying us, while still preserving our freedom of choice. At the same time He is developing an ironclad guarantee that once the problem is solved, it will never come up again. It's a pretty tall order; tall enough that we should be slow to criticize unless we think we could do it better ourselves.

God has it all figured out. If He allows sin to run its course just long enough that nobody has any lingering doubt that it's the wrong way to go, the problem will be solved. Have we reached that point as a society?

Given the number of people who are fully aware of the harsh consequences of lousy choices and are still making them, maybe not. But in the long run, most of us will have touched the hot stove enough to know *why* God said, "don't touch." Given the chance to leave misery behind, we won't want to touch it again.

It's as if God said to the devil, "Here's the plan. I'm going to let you run your program for a little while, so that everybody can see for themselves *why* I told them that following Me is just a better way to live. Lucifer, do your very best. Go build yourself an empire. And I'll allow the whole universe to see where your kind of self-sufficient rebellion really goes. In the end, everybody gets to decide who's telling the truth."

Sometimes, when you have your hands full with stubborn, rebellious children, and you want to save them for the long run, you have to let them hit rock bottom. You have to let them find out the hard way. And once the poison of rebellion had infected God's universe,

He knew the best way to put an end to the problem forever (without deliberately destroying us) was to let us find out for ourselves. God didn't *choose* sin for us; we did that all by ourselves. When we decided we didn't want to follow His advice or live by His rules, and we chose instead to follow another path, God decided to let us find out exactly where our choice would take us.

You'll notice, however, that He didn't leave us without direction. When Jesus was on Earth, He talked about showing people God's "name." In the Bible, names are more than mere labels; they actually tell you something about a person's character. That makes what Jesus says in His prayer to the Father significant:

I have manifested Your name to the men whom You have given Me out of the world. They were Yours, You gave them to Me, and they have kept Your word. (John 17:6)

What does Jesus mean when He says He showed God's "name" to the disciples? It means He showed them the *character* of God. When you look at Jesus, you get to see God. That's important to understand, because so many people draw a sharp distinction between the God of the Old Testament and Jesus of Nazareth. Jesus says that we have understood God wrongly, and part of His mission was to clear up the misunderstandings.

When you study the character of Christ, you see the character of *God.* And the longer you study Christ, the more you get this distinct feeling that someone has been lying to us about what God is really like. It turns out that He's not arbitrary or severe. He's not an isolationist who doesn't care about our fate. In the Person of Jesus Christ, we get to see the truth: God really *is* love. And His plan is to eradicate suffering forever:

What do you conspire against the Lord? He will make an utter end of it. Affliction will not rise up a second time. (Nahum 1:9)

And I saw a new heaven and a new earth, for the first heaven and the first earth had passed away. Also there was no more sea. Then I, John, saw the holy city, New Jerusalem, coming down out of heaven from God, prepared as a bride adorned for her husband. And I heard a loud voice from heaven saying, "Behold, the tabernacle of God is with men, and He will dwell with them, and they shall be His people, and God Himself will be with them and be their God. And God will wipe away every tear from their eyes; there shall be no more death, nor sorrow, nor crying; and there shall be no more pain, for the former things have passed away." Then He who sat on the throne said, "Behold, I make all things new." And He said to me, "Write, for these words are true and faithful." (Revelation 21:1-5)

Is evil real? No question about it. The Bible openly admits it, and reveals a breathtaking plan to eliminate it while preserving *us*. Skeptics may complain that they can't place their faith in something they can't *see*, but that's the point of Jesus Christ. Through His life and teachings, you *can* see what God is up to—and the prognosis is good. God *is* eliminating suffering: for good!

Darwinism, on the other hand, can't deal with the problem of evil at all. In the first place, it's hard to define what evil *is*, even though we all have this innate sense that it is real. Volumes have been written to explain how evolution gave us a sense of morality, but at the end of the day, all we have is a *sense* of morality. Morality doesn't really exist for the Darwinist, which becomes deeply unsatisfying ten minutes after terrorists fly planeloads of innocent passengers into the World Trade Center.

"But isn't the God of the Bible Himself one of the worst perpetrators of evil in the universe?"

I'll be honest; sometimes I get a little frustrated when I hear skeptics raise this question. On the one hand they complain about God's character when they perceive that God is doing nothing about the problem of evil, and then on the other, they complain when He does do something.

It's still a good question, though. What about all those times, particularly in the Old Testament, when God wiped out entire groups of people wholesale? Isn't that a violation of His own commandment against killing? Doesn't that put Him on the same level as Stalin or Hitler: either you play *my* way, or I'll wipe you out?

When you first stumble across one of these stories, you might be tempted to leap to that conclusion. But it's a little like starting to read *Old Yeller* at the end of the book: all you see is a boy shooting his dog. If that's all you know about the situation, you might have trouble believing that the boy loves his dog, or that his tears are heartfelt. Read the *whole* story, and you'll cry alongside the boy as he relieves the suffering of a dog hopelessly doomed by rabies. Anyone who has studied enough of the Bible will begin to cry alongside God

when entire groups of people have to be destroyed. The God of the
Bible just isn't like the gods of pagan mythology who toy with mortals
for sport. When God steps up to the plate, there's a *reason* for it. Pay
careful attention to the following accounts:

*Then the Lord saw that the wickedness of man was great in the earth, and
that every intent of the thoughts of his heart was only evil continually. And the
Lord was sorry that He had made man on the earth, and He was grieved in
His heart. So the Lord said, "I will destroy man whom I have created from the
face of the earth, both man and beast, creeping thing and birds of the air, for I
am sorry that I have made them." (Genesis 6:5-7)*

*Say to them: "As I live" says the Lord GOD, "I have no pleasure in the
death of the wicked, but that the wicked turn from his way and live. Turn, turn
from your evil ways! For why should you die, O house of Israel?"*
(Ezekiel 33:11)

Notice how God's personal agony rises to the surface in these
passages. He doesn't delight in death. It's not some sort of power
trip or vendetta against those who won't play nice. It's a last resort, a
desperate measure. God holds out as long as He can possibly tolerate
it before He does something dramatic. Why? The Bible makes it
clear:

*The Lord is not slack concerning His promise, as some count slackness,
but is longsuffering toward us, not willing that any should perish but that all
should come to repentance. But the day of the Lord will come as a thief in the
night, in which the heavens will pass away with a great noise, and the elements
will melt with fervent heat; both the earth and the works that are in it will be
burned up. (2 Peter 3:9, 10)*

An honest assessment of the scriptures reveals that God is loath
to destroy anything. We shouldn't forget, after all, that He is the
architect of creation, and what artist enjoys destroying his own work?
Yet certain situations demand that He intervene. In the destruction of
Sodom and Gomorrah, for example, the Bible makes it clear that the
situation had gotten out of hand:

*And the Lord said, "Because the outcry against Sodom and Gomorrah is
great, and because their sin is very grave, I will go down now and see whether
they have done altogether according to the outcry against it that has come to
Me; and if not, I will know." (Genesis 18:20, 21)*

While God is loath to destroy anyone, there comes a point where
He doesn't have any other option. When the infection of sin and

suffering becomes bad enough, you have to "put Old Yeller out of his misery."

The biblical command to destroy all of the Amalekites (1 Samuel 15:2, 3) falls into this category. Skeptics often point to this episode as proof positive that the God of the Bible is inconsistent at best, and a ruthless tyrant at worst. But nobody seems to ask *why* God might think it necessary.

It wasn't that He hated Amalekites. The Bible is clear that non-Hebrews were welcome to become a part of the nation of Israel. But God *did* hate their behavior, and He hated the potential for suffering that came as a result. Let's not forget who the Amalekites were:

Remember what Amalek did to you on the way as you were coming out of Egypt, how he met you on the way and attacked your rear ranks, all the stragglers at your rear, when you were tired and weary; and he did not fear God. (Deuteronomy 25:17, 18)

The Amalekites were determined to destroy Israel. They went out of their way to attack Israel shortly after the departure from Egypt, and their object of attack was the weak and tired at the rear of the procession. The Amalekites were hardly innocent bystanders. Apparently, their determination and wickedness had gone so far that there was little hope for a truce.

The Bible indicates that they received plenty of warning before they met their end, and they simply wouldn't change their ways. What option is left when you have a rabid dog that endangers everyone else? It's another case of Old Yeller.

Many of the Canaanite tribes had an incurable case of spiritual rabies. Their wickedness defies the imagination, even by today's standards. They engaged in unthinkably debased sex acts, and they sacrificed their children by placing them in the hands of a red-hot idol. They had become a blight on the world that was threatening to spread misery far and wide. And it should be noted that God always preserved those whose hearts were still open to Him before taking action,[29] which again indicates that He patiently and lovingly waits until someone has actually crossed the point of no return before He takes action to prevent their wickedness from spreading to others.

Let's suppose for a moment that God *never* dealt with the situation. Would we still call Him a God of love if He simply allowed wickedness and the resultant suffering to go on forever? Of course not.

"Christians claim that God hates sinners!"

Some people find the "wrath" of God a little confusing. We tend to project human qualities onto God when we think of Him getting angry. We compare His wrath against sin to some of the behaviors exhibited by so-called human representatives of God. When "Christian" organizations picket the funeral services of miners killed in an accident, shouting epithets and declaring that God willed their deaths because of homosexuality in America,[30] many non-Christians understandably identify their actions with the Christian religion and are turned off by it. In their minds, they associate that kind of behavior with the God of the Bible. But the behavior of a few unthinking extremists hardly represents the character of the Creator.

Does God get angry? There's no question about it. The Bible is replete with examples of God's fury against *sin*. But if God is just and fair, and really love, you wouldn't expect anything else. Parents should have an easy time understanding this. When children do things that endanger their well-being, it naturally upsets a parent, not because he or she suddenly hates the child, but because of the needless harm that befalls their offspring.

A father is angry because his son is in the hospital after being injured during a night of reckless street racing. A mother is angry when her child wanders off without telling her and she wasn't able to find him for hours.

Does God get angry about sin? Yes. Does that mean He hates us? Absolutely not. A bit of careful thought should sort this out. If God actually hated us, wouldn't He delight in the suffering we have to endure? Why would sin and suffering make Him angry if He didn't care? On Earth we understand that children sometimes push their parents' buttons to see if they're going to react. They want to know where the boundaries are. If their parents love them, they *expect* a reaction. If they get nothing in return for poor behavior, it sends a terrible message: *my Mom and Dad don't care*. If God *never* reacted to evil, we'd charge Him with not caring, too.

We've been far too quick to misjudge God's motives, painting a picture of a petty child who angrily grabs his ball and bat when the rest of the children won't play the way *he* wants. That's an unfair caricature of God based on human opinion instead of the weight of scriptural evidence.

"But God kills people!
That's a violation of His own commandment against killing!"

This is an understandable objection if you give the sixth commandment nothing but a cursory reading. It doesn't actually say, "you shall not *kill*," at least not in the original language. The Hebrew word for "kill" is *ratsach*, which is a reference to *murder* rather than any sort of killing. The essence of the commandment is that we cannot kill when we do not have the right to do so. In fact, some modern translations of the Bible render this commandment, "you shall not murder." There's a difference.

Does *God* have the right to terminate a life? Of course. He's the author of life; it belongs to Him. When He sees it necessary to intervene dramatically for the greater good (for example, to nip a serious situation in the bud or to preclude unacceptable levels of suffering), He has the right to make that call. We do not. And if you check the records, you'll find that God really *is* long-suffering; He always waits until all other options have been exhausted before He resorts to physically removing the problem.

CHAPTER SEVEN

Arguments Against the Existence of God

Number Four: The Argument from Multiplicity

This argument is rather simplistic and easy to refute. It essentially says that because there are so many religions and so many gods, the God of the Bible falls into the same category as the others. He is merely one more installment in our historical collection of myths. If there are so many gods, it is argued, then we cannot think that any of them are real.

Here's what's interesting about this sort of thinking in light of Darwinism. Evolutionists try to establish the case that religion, like everything else, has evolved over time. I have a number of books in my library that argue for monotheistic religion being a natural outgrowth of polytheistic religion. It is commonly asserted that man began to invent deities to explain natural phenomena: the god of rain, the god of thunder, the god of sunshine, etc. Over time, these many gods were lumped together in one all-powerful God. The Hebrews were among the first to move in this direction, and are often credited as being the first monotheists.

We have discovered, however, that the opposite is usually the case: polytheistic religions seem to have *de*volved from monotheistic beliefs. In other words, most cultures have gone from worshiping *one* God to worshiping *many* gods. This is the understanding presented in Paul's letter to the Romans:

For since the creation of the world His invisible attributes are clearly seen, being understood by the things that are made, even His eternal power and Godhead, so that they are without excuse, because, although they knew God, they did not glorify Him as God, nor were thankful, but became futile in their thoughts, and their foolish hearts were darkened. Professing to be wise, they became fools, and changed the glory of the incorruptible God into an image made like corruptible man—and birds and four-footed animals and creeping things. (Romans 1:20-23)

Workers in the mission fields of the world have discovered this biblical account to be perfectly accurate. Don Anderson's book, *Eternity in Their Hearts*, provides a number of stunning examples of non-Christian religions that have grown out of ancient monotheism.[31] Here is one such example:

In the far north of Burma, another half-million red-turbaned, fiercely independent people called the Kachin *also acknowledged their Creator. In their folk religion the Creator Being "whose shape or form exceeds man's ability to comprehend." Sometimes the Kachin called him* Hpan Wa Ningsang—*The Glorious One Who Creates, or* Che Wa Ningchang—*The One Who Knows.*

Dr. Herman Tegenfeldt, Ph.D., who lived among the Kachin for about 20 years and learned their language, wrote: "Kachin animists do not offer sacrifice to Karai Kasang, for as one Kachin put it, 'Why should we? He never did us any harm.' Nor is there any custom of worshiping him. However, in times of extreme need, when sacrifices to the spirits have brought no relief, Kachins are known to cry out to this distant Great Spirit." And the Kachin, like the Karen, believed that Karai Kasang once gave their forefathers a book which they lost. Kachin beliefs did not specify how the lost book would be returned to them, but apparently they were open to the possibility that it would be restored.[32]

Many more examples of so-called "pagan" religions that have retained a memory of the one true Creator God could be cited. In 1867, for example, Lars Skrefsrud and Hans Borreson traveled to India to preach the gospel to the Santal people. When they arrived, they made a remarkable discovery:

To Skrefsrud's utter amazement, the Santal were electrified almost at once by the gospel message. At length he heard Santal sages, including one named Kolean, exclaim, "What this stranger is saying must mean that Thakur Jiu has not forgotten us after all this time!"

Skrefsrud caught his breath in astonishment. Thakur *was a Santal word meaning "genuine."* Jiu *meant "god."*[33]

Not only did the Santal believe in a "Genuine God," the one true Creator, they also told a remarkable story about the origins of man. According to Santal legend, God first created a man and a woman, Haram and Ayo. A being named Lita tempted them to drink rice beer, and when they awoke from their drunken stupor they realized they were naked and felt ashamed. Later on, their descendants became so wicked that Thakur Jiu was forced to destroy them with a flood—but one family was hidden in a cave on Mount Harata. The Santal explained that they were descendants of the remaining family, but they had departed from the worship of Thakur Jiu many generations ago. They began to worship spirits instead.[34]

This story, which has been found in various forms all over the world, suggests the exact opposite of Darwinian explanations for religion. Mankind moved from monotheism to polytheism, not the other way around. The evolutionist theory suggests that religion has improved over time, moving from simplistic savagery and magic to the point where we are now sophisticated enough to give it up all together. The stories that linger among tribes of people who have never had contact with each other completely disagree with this premise. On the whole, religion has not *evolved*; it has *devolved*. As rebellion against God has taken its toll on the human race, we have actually regressed in our ethical standards.

I find it highly interesting that the story of Genesis portrays the original transgression of man as an attempt to step up to a higher plane of existence:

And the serpent said to the woman, "You will not surely die. For God knows that in the day you eat of it your eyes will be opened, and you will be like God, knowing good and evil." (Genesis 3:4, 5)

Eve is told she will ascend to greater heights if she transgresses the will of God; precisely the opposite happens. As a result of doubting God's Word and rebelling against Him, the human race sinks into a sewer of sin and misery.

Is it possible that the same sort of delusion invented by the serpent is being thrust upon us by Darwinians? Do we imagine mankind building a better religion all by himself, when in fact it has been in regression for years?

Why is it that virtually all over the world the human race has a memory of a better existence in the distant past? Does this make sense if we were once mere animals, scraping for existence in a brutal environment? Even the laws of nature tell us that left to itself, the universe moves toward chaos, not order. Energy is dissipating and the universe is winding down. It is one of the foundational laws of physics, and yet evolutionary biologists want us to believe that living organisms are making progress—all on their own. Chaos, they say, is giving rise to order, all by itself. Even though we've rejected God, we imagine ourselves becoming gods over millions of years.

Another form of the argument from multiplicity can be found among skeptics who point out the similarities between Judeo-Christian beliefs and ancient "pagan" religions. I can't argue that similarities don't exist, because they do. But I find the explanation given by the skeptics deeply unsatisfactory. They claim that the Bible borrowed from the polytheistic pagan religions that preceded them and used pagan mythology to fabricate a new religion.

Let me give an example. Critics sometimes point to things like the date we use for Christmas as evidence that we have constructed our religion on the ruins of paganism, and at first glance, they seem to have a point. We know—beyond the shadow of a doubt—that Christ was *not* born on December 25. In all likelihood He was born some time in the spring. We also know that December 25 was used by pagan religions as a high holy day many years before the birth of Christ. What one is expected to believe is that Christians therefore fabricated this holiday and tried to pass it off as biblical fact.

However, no skeptic has yet been able to point to the passage of scripture that gives us the date of Christ's birth. All the Bible tells us is that Christ *was* born, not *when*. The authors of the Bible did *not* borrow their religion from the pagans. Later Christians, however, *did* occasionally import pagan elements into their Christian faith, and there's a difference. God cannot be said to be the author of those changes, and neither can the scriptures.

Don't forget the world into which the Christian church was born. It was ruled by the pagan Roman Empire, which for the first few centuries of Christianity persecuted the church ruthlessly. Then in the year 312 A.D., the Roman emperor Constantine supposedly had a vision on his way to the Battle of Milvian Bridge, in which he saw the shape of the cross superimposed on the sun. A voice told him, "in hoc signes vinces," or "in this sign conquer." When he won the battle, he assumed that the Christian God had told him to convert and fight all his future battles under the sign of the cross.

The effect Constantine's conversion had on the world is hard to overestimate. Suddenly, the Christian church was no longer an outcast in the Roman Empire; it became the religion of the state. Instead of persecuting Christians, Constantine (who had worshiped the sun as his primary deity up to this point) now *encouraged* people to become Christians. One account even has Constantine marching his armies through the Tiber River in order to "baptize" them as Christians.

The problem was that many of the "conversions" were far from sincere. It became economically and socially convenient to call oneself a Christian, and before long, the original faith of the Christians had been compromised with pagan teachings that were imported into the church with the new "believers."

Admittedly, this is a rather simplistic account of what happened, but because this is not primarily a book on European history, it will suffice for our purposes. Many pagan traditions were simply carried over into the Christian church, including the observance of the 25th of December. The rationale was that each pagan tradition that was continued in the Christian community would be "whitewashed" and reinterpreted to give it a Christian meaning. Voila! Jesus was now considered to born on the 25th of December.

Does this minor change discredit the Christian religion? Hardly. Nor has it substantially changed the religion itself. Christianity—as Christ intended it—is still found in the pages of the Bible, intact and unchanged. Our practice of the religion may become misguided from time to time, but the Divine yardstick has not moved.

Are there pagan elements in the modern practice of Christianity? Yes. But most of the time, when you notice a striking resemblance to ancient pagan religions, you will discover that the practice has been imported by people rather than decreed by the scriptures. Most of these changes have been harmless. Some have not (but that is a subject for another book).

The fact that we have many forms of religion on the planet simply does not preclude the idea that one of them might be right. In the oversensitive and politically correct atmosphere we live in at the moment, it may be uncomfortable to suggest that one religion might be right at the expense of others, but that doesn't mean it isn't true. Logic alone tells you that disagreement doesn't void everyone's viewpoint. Someone might actually be right.

CHAPTER EIGHT

Arguments Against the Existence of God

Number Five: The Argument from Irreducible Complexity

Our discussion of God's existence now takes us directly into the realm of Darwinian evolution. You'll notice that up to this point we've been dealing with the arguments *against* God's existence, and for good reason. I am persuaded that the theory of evolution is not merely the product of dispassionate scientific observation; it is, rather, a calculated argument against God's existence. Of course, some might wonder what the arguments *for* God's existence are. Over the centuries there have been a number of notable attempts to defend God's existence by means of philosophical reasoning.

One of the earliest (at least in Western Civilization) was the **ontological** argument, developed by the medieval philosopher Anselm of Canterbury. His argument ran like this:

- God is that of which no greater can be conceived.
- If God exists only in my imagination, then it is possible
  to conceive of a greater God, one that exists in reality.
- Therefore, God must be real.

As much as I *want* Anselm to be right, I have to admit that's a pretty lousy argument. First of all, it all hinges on his personal definition of God rather than on the description of God's nature available in scripture. Secondly, as a French monk by the name of Gaunilon pointed out, the argument falls apart when you replace God with anything else. He chose to use an island to demonstrate the fallacy of Anselm's reasoning:

- Imagine an island so perfect that you can't think of
  one more perfect.
- If that island only exists in my imagination, then it is possible

to conceive of a *more* perfect island, one that exists in reality.
- Therefore, the perfect island must be real.

Illogical? Of course. It simply doesn't work, and we really don't need to spend much more time on this argument, because it's been so thoroughly refuted over the centuries.

A second argument, first presented by Plato and Aristotle, but developed by Thomas Aquinas, is the **first cause argument.** Aquinas reasoned that as we study nature we observe the law of cause and effect. Everything that happens in this world has a cause, and in turn, the cause itself was caused by something else. For example, we know that rain is caused by moisture in the air cooling and condensing. How did the moisture get into the air? Through the process of evaporation. What caused evaporation? The heat of the sun. What caused the heat of the sun? The complex nuclear furnace the sun is made of. And what caused that? *Et cetera.*

Aquinas argued that as you trace back through all the causes in the universe, you will ultimately discover the *first cause*, which is God. And what caused God? He is *un*caused—a concept supported by scripture. He has simply always been there:

Before the mountains were brought forth, or ever You had formed the earth and the world, even from everlasting to everlasting, You are God.
(Psalm 90:2)

Doubtless You are our Father, though Abraham was ignorant of us, and Israel does not acknowledge us. You, O Lord, are our Father; our Redeemer from Everlasting is Your name. (Isaiah 63:16)

It's interesting that this sort of thinking still drives the practice of science today, even though a lot of scientists seem to be working hard to disprove the existence of God. Why do we even have science? Because we believe that something *caused* the phenomena around us. We want to know what *causes* the northern lights. We want to know what *causes* energy so we can harness it. We believe that the world around us has a *cause*—but then stop short of suggesting there is a deliberate *first cause* because of the moral implications.

Prominent evolutionists will argue, in fact, that actual day-to-day process of evolution does not occur by blind chance but because of a naturally occurring order of cause and effect. It is only the *origin* of everything around us that is said to have happened by random chance. In essence, everything has a cause except the big bang, which just happened. When Edwin Hubble and others started suggesting that the universe actually had a beginning, scientists became uncomfortable because of the implications. What put the big bang in place? Who set up the laws? The whole thing was becoming a little too close to looking like God for many of them.

What is interesting is that notable atheists like Richard Dawkins have tried to take the argument from cause and effect and turn it on its head in order to eliminate God from the picture once again. He argues that if we're going to say that it is improbable that our universe came into existence all by itself, then we must also say that God is improbable because we cannot discern *His* origin:

However statistically improbable the entity you seek to explain by invoking a designer, the designer himself has got to be at least as improbable.[35]

Apparently it's logical to ignore the laws of probability and suggest that the universe got started by accident, but illogical to suggest that God started it because we cannot figure out how God Himself got started!

To be honest, I can't explain the existence of God, because it's out of my grasp—but it's high time that evolutionists admit that they also have a few question marks at the beginning of their evolutionary charts. They *hypothesize* that it all started with the "big bang," but they can't tell you *why* the so-called big bang happened.

They also can't tell you *why* evolution works. Why is it that organisms *improve* over time, and move toward higher and higher life forms? What mysterious rules keep the process moving in one direction? Why isn't life *devolving*, and degenerating into *lower* life forms? When the reptile became a bird, why didn't he next start moving backwards to become a fish?

"That's just not the way it works!" Well, why not? What is it that is supposedly *causing* evolution to move in a certain direction? "We don't know!" But that response is considered invalid when Christians are asked where God comes from, or how He could exist without beginning.

This, of course, brings us to perhaps the most popular defense of the existence of God, the **Intelligent Design Argument.** Not only does everything have a *cause*, but it also works so well that it appears to have been designed on purpose.

John O'Keefe, a planetary scientist with NASA from 1958 to 1995, put it like this:

We are, by astronomical standards, a pampered, cosseted, cherished group of creatures.... If the Universe had not been made with the most exacting precision we could never have come into existence. It is my view that these circumstances indicate the universe was created for man to live in.[36]

It's a very compelling argument. Should conditions on Earth be even a little bit different, we simply couldn't survive. A 1997 article in *The Wall Street Journal* expressed it well:

...in recent decades, physicists have noticed an astonishing thing about the fundamental laws of nature. The 20 or so parameters they contain—numbers governing the strength of gravity, the ratio of the proton's size to the neutron's, and so on—appear to have been fine-tuned so that, against astronomically unfavorable odds, conscious organisms could emerge. Make gravity the slightest bit weaker, and no galaxies suitable for life would have formed; make it the slightest bit stronger and the cosmos would have collapsed upon itself moments after the big bang.[37]

Of course, evolutionists have attempted to answer the apparent design of the universe by appealing to probability. They recognize that the odds of our universe coming into existence by chance, along with all the life it supports, are astronomically *against* their suggestion. Their solution? Give it enough time and the improbable can happen!

Can this really happen? Well, we're here, aren't we? As Douglas Adams (famous atheist and author of the *Hitchhiker's Guide to the Galaxy*) put it, the accidental origins of the universe aren't *impossible*, they're just *improbable*.

I beg to differ. For generations, scientists believed in the theory of spontaneous generation. When the Nile River flooded, we observed that wet dust produces frogs. When maggots appeared in a piece of rotting meat, it was explained that rotting meat gives birth to maggots. It wasn't until 1668 that somebody challenged this kind of thinking. Francesco Redi argued that maggots came from flies' eggs, not from rotting meat. He proved it by isolating the meat so that flies could not reach it, and no maggots appeared. His theory? *Life cannot come from non-life.* Nobody believed him. Almost two hundred years later, Louis Pasteur proved it in the laboratory, and now we know it to be a law of nature.

The theory of evolution however, asks us to suspend this law and accept that life really *did* come from non-life. Gases and minerals somehow combined to form living things. Even though it has never happened in the present age, and we have failed to make it happen in the laboratory, we are asked to believe that life on Earth just spontaneously generated from non-living matter. In any discipline outside of evolutionary "science," this is known to be impossible.

Perhaps this was more believable a century and a half ago. Ernst Haeckel, for example, believed that cells were essentially organic blobs of jelly, and he suggested that the right combination of chemicals could have accidentally produced them and given rise to living organisms. In his opinion, living cells were simple chemical cocktails that could have occurred quite by accident, given the right chemical soup millions of years ago.

In the 1950s, Stanley Miller of the University of Chicago tried to reproduce the atmospheric conditions he believed existed on Earth just prior to the emergence of simple life forms. He pushed methane, ammonia, water vapor and hydrogen through a glass chamber where he exposed them to high-voltage electrical charges to simulate the effect that solar radiation might have had on the ancient atmosphere of Earth. After working for a couple of days, Miller discovered trace amounts of amino acids at the bottom of the chamber. He trumpeted his find as proof that life emerged on its own.

The real problem with his discovery, frankly, is that an amino acid is *not* life. No scientist has yet to produce actual *life* in the laboratory. We might clone animals or revive nearly-dead people, but we do not have the ability to create life. And life simply does *not* come from non-life, not in our laboratories, and certainly not by accident.

Subsequent study has demonstrated that the earliest atmosphere of Earth was not like Miller imagined. According to Stephen C. Meyer, "...new geological and geochemical evidence suggests that prebiotic atmospheric conditions were hostile, not friendly to the production of amino acids and other essential building blocks of life."[38] Furthermore, a careful study of the geological record has failed to provide any evidence whatsoever of the existence of a "primordial broth" at any point in the Earth's history.

One of the key reasons we were quick to adopt the idea that simple cellular life could emerge on its own is precisely because we thought it was *simple.* We can overlook Haeckel's error on the grounds that he couldn't actually *see* what we can now observe going on at the cellular level. Now that we've seen it, we no longer have an excuse.

In fact, the more we study life at the cellular level, the more we realize that cells are *irreducibly complex.* That means that we can't possibly conceive of any mechanism by which they gradually developed, because the parts are so intricate and interdependent that it is incomprehensible that any of them could have possibly evolved on their own. Individual parts need other parts in order to function, and if anything is missing, the cell's functions utterly break down.

Years of experimentation and research have forced scientists to admit, by and large, that they don't know much about the origin of life. What we're finding under the microscope is far more advanced than we originally suspected, and it defies a simple explanation. Meyer states it like this:

...the revolution in the field of molecular biology has revealed so great a complexity and specificity of design in even the simplest cells and cellular components as to defy materialistic explanation. Even scientists known for a staunch commitment to materialistic philosophy now concede that materialistic science in no way suffices to explain the origin of life.... As origin-of-life biochemist Klaus Dose has said, "More than 30 years of experimentation on the origin of life in the fields of chemical and molecular evolution have led to a better perception of the immensity of the problem of the origin of life on Earth rather than to its solution. At present all discussions on principle theories and experiments in the field either end in stalemate or confession of ignorance."[39]

Does the theory of evolution explain the incredible complexity of the world around us? Can it explain those parts of living organisms that need all of their components to function? Hardly. As science progresses we are being forced to admit that there seems to have been a deliberately designed set of blueprints for life on planet Earth. Robert Jastrow, the famous astronomer and physicist, is reportedly an agnostic who is baffled by the mystery of origins. His study of astronomy, however, led him to make this important observation back in 1978:

For the scientist who has lived by his faith in the power of reason, the story ends like a bad dream. He has scaled the mountains of ignorance; he is about to conquer the highest peak; as he pulls himself over the final rock, he is greeted by a band of theologians who have been sitting there for centuries.[40]

What is science discovering? The closer it looks, the more complex the universe becomes. It's getting very difficult to say it was an accident.

Interestingly, Richard Dawkins has used the arguments of first cause and irreducible complexity to attack belief in God. In his opinion, these arguments actually *disprove* the existence of God rather than suggest it. The essence of his argument is this:

• Christians point out that everything has a cause, and that something was the first cause of everything. Therefore God exists. But this is an inadequate explanation, because it leaves unresolved the origin of God Himself. Who created God?

• Christians say that some things in nature are irreducibly complex, like some of the functions in a cell. Take away any portion of the apparatus that makes something happen, and the cell would cease to be able to survive. Therefore evolution by slow degrees cannot be true, because the cell must exist complete with all of its advanced parts, to survive. In turn, Dawkins says irreducible complexity cannot be a good argument, because God Himself would be irreducibly complex and therefore cannot have an origin.

Does this argument knock the feet out from under a belief in God? Hardly. In his analysis, Dawkins makes one critical oversight: God is not the same as His creation, and we should not expect to evaluate Him on the same basis we evaluate the world around us.

Let me see if I can explain. When I walk into an art gallery and see the works of Pablo Picasso, I instinctively understand that someone intelligent designed those paintings. Nobody would believe that they came about as the result of an elephant stomping through paint and then trotting across a field of blank canvases. They are clearly *not* the product of chance.

Let's suppose I am ignorant of how they came into existence, however, and I ask the director of the gallery about their origin. "They were created," he says, "when Mr. Picasso was inspired and put his brush to the canvases."

"But that can't be!" I cry, exasperated. "Because then who in the world painted Mr. Picasso in the first place?"

Do you see it? Picasso *isn't a painting*, and God *is not a creation*. Picasso was a *painter*, and God is a *creator*. You don't apply the same rules to the painter as the painting, because they are not the same.

When we argue that God cannot possibly exist because He doesn't have an identifiable first cause, or because He is Himself irreducibly complex, we are trying to compare apples and oranges. The rules don't apply. In fact, He *made* the rules.

And to suggest that irreducible complexity is not a good defense of creation because God Himself is irreducible is the height of absurdity. God describes Himself as being from "everlasting." He was not created. Of course He is irreducibly complex. He does not rely on time and space in the same way we do for existence. Dawkins simply rejects this because he does not understand *how* that could be. But I would suggest that Mr. Dawkins couldn't possibly reject everything he doesn't understand, even in the realm of science. He is just rejecting that which invades his personal philosophy.

At best, this kind of reasoning is a last-ditch attempt to hang on to the idea that the universe is a happy (or not-so-happy, depending on your point of view) accident. To suggest that God must be created Himself in order to exist is simply arrogant thinking that supposes mankind already knows everything there is to know. We believe that if God exists, *we* should be able to explain Him. But if we could completely explain God, that would put us somewhere above Him, and He emphatically states that's not the case. And He should know— after all, He designed our brains in the first place.

CHAPTER NINE

A Parade of Pretenders

Finding Our Roots

For many, many centuries, human beings have been happy to explore the surface of the planet, discovering mysterious new lands and sailing uncharted waters. In the last few hundred years, however, we broke away from mere horizontal exploration to venture in new directions: the ocean floor and the cosmos.

So far we have discovered no humanoid life forms in either of those places. When the disciplines of archaeology and geology began to flourish, we *did* find something buried in the ground, however: remains that look a little like people.

Back in 1869, two men digging a well on a farm in upstate New York stumbled across something remarkable buried in the earth: a human leg. Quickly forgetting the well, they feverishly dug until the rest of the body was excavated. It was more than ten feet long.

Word of the discovery spread quickly, and within a matter of days, wagons started arriving from all over the state, bringing a wide array of people who wanted to see the body. Each visitor was charged twenty-five cents to see it, and when the crowds refused to let up, the price of admission was doubled to fifty cents. In no time at all, the owners of the giant cadaver had grossed more than $30,000—a considerable sum in the mid-nineteenth century.

As the money continued to roll in, other people started to realize the financial potential of owning a dead giant. To give you an idea of how much money was being generated by the giant, consider the offers that William Newell, owner of the farm, *turned down*. A neighbor offered him the deed to his farm in exchange for the body. P. T. Barnum offered $60,000 just to *rent* the body for three months. Both men were refused.

Quite apart from its monetary value, the body was creating quite a stir among those who were trying to figure out just who or what the buried giant was. After visiting the Newell farm, E. W. Leavenworth, the Secretary of State for New York, said, "It has the mark of ages stamped upon every limb and feature, in a manner and with a distinctness which no art can imitate." Experts scrambled to find an explanation of the massive human remains. Some believed it to be a petrified corpse; others though it was a statue, a relic of a long-lost civilization.

When P. T. Barnum failed to obtain the Cardiff Giant, as it came to be called, he had a counterfeit made that he quickly put on display. He claimed that Newell had sold it to him and that the giant on display on Newell's farm was a fake. As it turns out, *both* of them were fakes.

The original Cardiff Giant was carved from a twelve-foot block of gypsum by a team of marble cutters in Chicago at the request of George Hull, a man who wanted to convince the clergymen of the day that it was an authentic find. Once the statue had been carved, it was severely etched with acid and scored with needles to make it look ancient, and then it was buried on Newell's farm about a year before it was discovered.

P. T. Barnum was right. There *is* a sucker born every minute. (There is evidence to suggest that it was actually George Hull's business partner who coined that phrase, not Barnum.) We look back on the story of the Cardiff Giant with a smile on our faces, because of all those poor, naive people who paid good money to stand in line for nothing.

Could it be that *we* are standing in just such a line ourselves? On a regular basis, people claim to find a new human ancestor buried in the ground, from Lucy in Africa to the "hobbit" man of Southeast Asia. Even though a majority of Americans still believe in a Creator God (a fact that appalls men like Richard Dawkins), there is still a lot of credence given to the idea that we may have descended from distinctly more rudimentary primate life forms.

While it is considered something of an oversimplification to say we "come from monkeys," the theories presented for our consideration don't fall far from that idea. It is routinely pointed out that we have a significant amount of DNA in common with chimpanzees, and it is suggested that we parted company with them anywhere from

4-7 million years ago. While evolutionists do *not* say we came from monkeys, they *do* believe we are closely related and have common ancestors.

Where does the proof come from? The ground.

One of the first discoveries occurred in 1891, when Eugene Dubois unearthed human-like remains on the East Indian island of Java. His find has come to be known as *Java Man* (Pithecanthropus erectus.) It was considered a breakthrough find, because Darwinists had failed to produce any fossils demonstrating our supposed descent from primates. If, as Darwin suggested, we had evolved over millions of years from ape-like creatures, there should be some evidence of it in the fossil record. Until Java Man, there was none.

The evolutionist community naturally got excited. Here was proof that man had come from other life forms! Java Man clearly had features that were *almost* human and *almost* ape,

What, exactly, did Dubois find? A skullcap and three teeth. No complete skeleton—not even the majority of one. Just a skullcap and three teeth, each of which appeared to belong to an ape. So how do you claim human ancestry for this creature? From a human thighbone he found at the same site. The only problem with the femur was that he found it a year later—fifty feet away from the original find.

Dubois simply took the skullcap of an ape and the thighbone of a human being and put them together, declaring that he had discovered an ape-man. It immediately raises some obvious questions, however: how did that leg bone end up fifty feet away? And what linked it to the skullcap? Apparently it was linked by *assumption*. Dubois personally believed that there were no humans on the island at the time the bones were originally buried. And, in his thinking, if there were no humans, then the leg bone must belong to an ape.

In 1907, a German expedition, known as the Selenka Expedition, returned to the island hoping to prove the authenticity of Java Man. They excavated more than 10,000 cubic meters of soil, down to a depth of more than thirty-six feet. They collected forty-three boxes of fossilized bones.

What they discovered completely discredited Dubois. Both human and ape fossils were found in the same geological stratum, proving that apes and men had once cohabited the island. They also discovered that the whole region had been victim to a volcanic eruption sometime in the relatively recent past. As lava and volcanic ash swept over the area, it buried a number of people and animals simultaneously. The skullcap unearthed by Dubois belonged to an ape, and the leg bone belonged to a human. A 342-page report stated that Java Man wasn't a man at all, and had played absolutely no part in the development of the human race.

In 1920, Dubois confessed that he had found two fully human skulls at the same spot where he had unearthed the ape's skullcap. To defend his faith in Darwin, Dubois had chosen to misrepresent his findings.

A third expedition went to the site in 1931, led by G. H. R. von Koenigswald. As he searched the area, he discovered several human skulls, but absolutely no intermediate or transitory life forms between man and ape. A shortage of funds due to the Great Depression forced him to abandon his search, but when he returned in 1938, he discovered more ape-like skullcaps and became excited enough to declare that he had found more examples of Java Man.

But when others reviewed his findings and examined the skullcap fragments carefully, they found them to be very much like the one Dubois had found, and declared that they belonged to either a chimpanzee or a gibbon. By this time, Dubois was reconsidering his original proclamation. He realized that the ancient burial ground in Java had both human *and* ape remains, but no hybrids. It was simply a volcanic disaster site. Java Man was not a man at all.

The sad part of the saga of the Java Man is that while those who made the discoveries have admitted that Java Man is not what they had hoped, he still continues to make appearances in textbooks and respected magazines. But Java Man has never existed in any place *except* an article. He is a figment of our imagination.

As doubts about Java Man started to circulate, a new intermediate life form appeared on the horizon to take his place: *Piltdown Man*. In December 1912, Sir Arthur Woodward of the British Museum and Charles Dawson announced to a distinguished audience that they had found some unusual fossilized remains at Piltdown Common. The crowd was astounded: a human-like skull with an ape-like jawbone had been unearthed. They were, of course, ecstatic, because they had at long last found the missing link. It was named *Eoanthropus Dawsoni*, in honor of Dawson.

It didn't take long for someone to throw a wet blanket on the party, however, because two men suddenly surfaced who claimed they walked in on Charles Dawson one day as he was busy staining bones in his office. Was Piltdown Man a fake?

The British Parliament apparently didn't think so. Through the Nature Conservancy, they pushed to have Piltdown Commons designated a national monument in honor of the important find. The claims of the two witnesses were quietly pushed aside.

Then in 1953, two British scientists managed to gain access to the bones, which had been locked away in the British Museum for decades. As they examined them they discovered that they were not ancient relics at all, but relatively modern bones that had been stained with bichromate to make them look ancient. When they examined the teeth, they found that they belonged to an orangutan and were covered with suspicious looking file marks. One author describes what they found:

The file marks on the orangutan teeth of the lower jaw were clearly visible. The molars were misaligned and filed at two different angles. The canine tooth had been filed down so far that the pulp cavity had been exposed and then plugged.[41]

Java Man had been helped along by a cover-up and an active imagination. Piltdown Man was a deliberate fraud. Someone had gone to great lengths to manufacture a missing link because Darwinism was in desperate need of one. Only those parts of the skull and jaw were included that made it impossible to determine the actual shape, size, or brain capacity. The bones were placed in a plaster cast in such a way that the skull was made to look bigger than an ape's, but smaller than a human's. It was fabricated so cleverly that most observers were convinced it was something between man and ape—a distant primate relative.

Unfortunately, Darwinian fabrications have a nasty habit of sticking around for a very long time. The creators of Piltdown Man pulled the wool over our eyes for forty years. Sadly, he survived a little longer in some school textbooks.

Today you could fill a large room with all of the books and articles written to prove its authenticity, including something like five hundred doctrinal dissertations. Proponents of the theory of evolution desperately needed something to prop up their sagging theory. After forty years, they discovered that the missing link was still missing.

Of course, evolutionists could always turn to *Nebraska Man*, who had been discovered in 1922. Realistically, to say that Nebraska "Man" had been discovered is overstating the case. The only thing actually discovered was a *tooth*. It wasn't a skeleton, a skull, or even *teeth*. Just one tooth. Professor Henry Osborne at the Natural History Museum in New York looked it over and declared that it was from an ancient primate ancestor of the human race.

Quite a number of scientists rushed to support Dr. Osborne's conclusion. In no time at all, believers imagined the rest of Nebraska Man; first a skull, then a full skeleton, and then a *face*. Then, on June 24, an artist's rendition of Nebraska Man made it into the *Illustrated London News*, which showed the prehistoric man living with his wife in their ancient habitat. All of this from a single tooth!

It's easy for us to forget just how widely the discovery of Nebraska Man was trumpeted. One of the men who had discovered the tooth was knighted by the King of England for his important contribution to natural history. At the famous Scopes Monkey Trail in 1925, William Jennings Bryan was confronted by a panel of scientists led by Professor H. H. Newman of the University of Chicago. Bryan had made the assertion that there was no evidence in the fossil record of intermediary life forms, so Professor Newman dazzled the courtroom with the "indisputable" proof of Nebraska Man.

Nebraska Man found his way into evolutionary charts drawn up by some very influential Darwinists. Dr. William Gregory, professor of paleontology at Columbia University, named him *Hesperopithecus*, and gave him a place of honor at the bottom of man's evolutionary tree at a meeting of the Philosophical Society of Philadelphia.

It turns out that he promoted the single tooth a little too quickly. A short time after the original discovery, geologist Harold Cook found another tooth just like the first one—but this time, there was a skeleton attached to it. Was the Darwin camp excited? Hardly. The skeleton wasn't human. It wasn't even primate. It was a peccary, a wild pig that still roams the woods of Paraguay to this day.

But they still had an Ace up their sleeve: *Neanderthal Man*. Of all the ape-men proposed by Darwinists, this is the one you probably remember best; today's textbooks still show pictures of a dim-witted-looking fellow with curved thighs and a massive eyebrow ridge. His bones were found in the Neander Valley in Germany back in 1856.

The first descriptions of Neanderthal Man were very convincing: He was as much primate as human, and had a much smaller brain capacity than ours. Perhaps we had evolved from *him!* Then Marcellin Boule measured the skull carefully. It turns out that, on average, Neanderthal Man had a brain capacity 13 percent *larger* than ours. Are we now to believe that we have actually *de*volved from Neanderthal Man?

Further examination of the site revealed that not only was Neanderthal man intelligent, but he also believed in the supernatural and buried his dead using elaborate ceremonies. He was a skilled craftsman who used tools, wore jewelry, and made musical instruments. There is even some evidence to suggest that he intermarried with human beings who look like us; modern human remains have been found buried with Neanderthal remains. This obviously poses problems for those who would like to claim Neanderthal man as forerunner to modern humans. If he was our ancestor, how did we end up in the same grave? Clearly, we *coexisted* with them.

Still, were they some sort of ape-man race who differed from us? Those who have conducted DNA testing on their remains would have us believe so. In 1997 the journal *Cell* published an article by a team of researchers entitled *Neanderthal DNA Sequences and the Origin of Modern Humans.* They explained how they had extracted mitochondrial DNA (mtDNA) from the arm of a Neanderthal fossil and subjected it to tests.[42] The researchers found smaller variations between modern humans than between modern humans and Neanderthals. The conclusion: Neanderthals are *not* our ancestors, but a separate line of "human" beings.[43] Dr. Burt Thompson disagrees with the finding:

The results of mtDNA research do not "show clearly that Neandertal was not our direct ancestor." Truth be told, a closer examination of the mtDNA research shows that it is not all it has been cracked up to be. The Krings study compared various DNA sequences from 1669 modern humans with one Neanderthal. Statistically, this not only is insignificant, but also incorrect. As Lubenow wrote in regard to this mtDNA research:

"Statistics has been used to cloud the relationship between Neanderthals and modern humans. It is improper to use statistical 'averages' in situations where many entities are being compared with only one entity. In this case, 994

sequences from 1669 modern humans are compared with one sequence from one Neanderthal. Thus, there is no Neanderthal 'average,' and the comparison is not valid (1998, 12[1]:92, emphasis added)." [44]

Is Neanderthal Man enough to build a case for our primate heritage? Hardly. He was *human*. So much so that we have found examples of what seem to be hybrids; remains that have both "human" and "Neanderthal" characteristics. Did he look different from you or I? Maybe. But the difference would have been no more striking than some of the physiological differences between the various strains of humans today.

When the first remains of Neanderthal Man were discovered outside of Düsseldorf, Dr. Rudolph Virchow said it appeared to be the body of a man who had suffered from rickets and osteoporosis. Rickets is a vitamin D deficiency that can result in bone malformations similar to those found in Neanderthal remains. There's a good chance, apart from their particular maladies, that Neanderthals may have looked a great deal like us.

At any rate, we know for a fact that they coexisted with modern humans, which rules them out as our progenitor. For whatever reason—disease, inbreeding, etc.—their appearance may have differed from ours. The diminutive Pygmies of Central Africa differ in appearance from the tall, slender Tutsi tribes that live just to the east of them. But both are distinctly human, and they coexist. Neanderthal Man was one of us.

The evolutionary camp has posited other candidates for "the missing link", but so far all of them have failed to provide any real evidence that human beings descended from anything other than human beings. *Rhodesian Man* was discovered in 1921, but also turned out to be fully human. *Taung African Man*, unearthed in 1924, proved to be the skull of a young ape.

Peking Man was once thought to be a prehistoric human skull, albeit a little smashed-in. However, it was found in a place where the ancient custom was to smash in a monkey's head to eat the brains; Peking Man turned out to be somebody's lunch.

Of course, no list of candidates for the missing link should leave out Lucy, the ancient half-man, half-ape discovered in Africa. How do we "know" that Lucy was an intermediary life form? Researchers used the ratio of leg and arm lengths to determine that she was not quite ape and not quite human. Very convincing, except for one problem. Take a look at a picture of Lucy and you'll notice that all of the bones are seriously fragmented, and it's impossible to be certain what the leg-to-arm length ratios really are. Someone has read something into Lucy's remains that may not actually be there! It should also be pointed out that Lucy's remains were found scattered across too improbable a distance to be certain they all came from the same organism. Today many experts are convinced Lucy was an ape.

By the time this book goes to press it's possible other contenders will be found. But, as with the other missing links, they won't hold out much hope for those who need to believe that we came from anywhere or anything other than God. Back in 1981 John Reader pointed out that not many fossil hominids (ape-like men) have held the spotlight for very long:

By now, laymen could be forgiven for regarding each new arrival as no less ephemeral than the weather forecast.[45]

The theory of human evolution from lower life forms might provide an exciting and imaginative foundation for science fiction movies like *Planet of the Apes,* but as the discovery of real evidence for human evolution seems less promising with each passing year, I wonder when we're finally going to admit we do not have sufficient data to support the hypothesis. Good science says it's time to let the hypothesis die. There simply aren't any transitional fossils that demonstrate man's evolution from lower beings.

I confess that I struggle to understand why some people are so desperate to discredit the Genesis account of origins. Why do we not want a Creator? Is it really better to propagate a theory that hasn't produced any real evidence in more than 150 years? If we don't have the evidence—solid evidence—why do we continue down this path?

I have heard some individuals vehemently argue that fossils are exceedingly rare, so finding the missing link is difficult; that's why we do not have it in our possession. It may be true that a minimal number of corpses actually fossilize, but I certainly do not agree that fossils are rare. There are millions of them all around us. I was able to travel down many of the country roads of my hometown and find fossils in the shale at the side of the road. In fact, there was a good-sized fossil bed about half an hour into the forest from where I lived, and I used to pull all kinds of fossils out of that hill.

They were mostly things I recognized: frogs, fish, leaves, ferns, bugs and shellfish—thousands of them. A few miles further away, others discovered things that weren't so familiar: the fossilized remains of mammoths and dinosaurs. What seems to be missing from the fossil record, however, are those all-important intermediary animals that would prove life on Earth has descended from other life forms. Most importantly, nobody has found the animal *we* supposedly came from. It exists only in the minds of those who choose to believe based on a handful of inconclusive bones.

The reason for the lack of evidence is remarkably simple: in the animal kingdom, like begets like. Puppies do not have kittens, tigers do not have calves, and monkeys do not have humans. A. H. Clark, a biologist on the staff of the Smithsonian, once wrote:

From all the tangible evidence that we now have been able to discover, we are forced to the conclusion that all the major groups of animals at the very first held just about the same relation to each other that they do today.[46]

All the major groups of animals have maintained the same relationship to each other from the very first. Crustaceans have always been crustaceans, echinoderms have always been echinoderms, and mollusks have always been mollusks. There is not the slightest evidence which supports any other viewpoint.[47]

Admittedly, his statements date back a number of decades, but I include them because not much has changed in the years since they were written. We have not discovered any transitory life forms, particularly between primate and human. Like simply gives birth to like, a scientific law ratified by scripture itself:

And God made the beast of the earth according to its kind, cattle according to its kind, and everything that creeps on the earth according to its kind. And God saw that it was good. Then God said, "Let Us make man in Our image, according to Our likeness; let them have dominion over the fish of the sea, over the birds of the air, and over the cattle, over all the earth and over every creeping thing that creeps on the earth." (Genesis 1:25, 26)

It's important not to miss the impact of what this verse is saying. Animals produce their own kind. God did not create some species of animal to eventually turn into another species. Any genetic mutation that we've been able to witness in the animal kingdom has been a tragic disaster rather than some sort of advantageous survival mechanism, and the mutants quickly die off. Not one genuinely beneficial mutation has been observed. Within their species, animals are locked into what they are. There is great variation and even observable change within a given species, as with the countless breeds of dogs that exist—but no matter what different dogs look like, they are all still dogs. They're not changing into elephants, and they didn't come from snails.

We should also take note of the fact that human beings are singled out in this passage as being different from the rest of the creation. Having been raised in a Christian home, I actually remember cringing when a teacher instructed us that human beings were members of the animal kingdom. I felt uncomfortable relegating people to simple mammals, because the Bible set us apart. In adulthood that same discomfort has been reborn when I hear people being lumped in with the animal kingdom, even though scientifically I understand why we have been classified that way.

But the Bible elevates us above the rest of creation (a fact that understandably makes some environmentalists uncomfortable when they see Christians abuse this arrangement) by saying that we are made in the image of God. Other animals look like their species. We, to some extent, look like God. We are *His* children. And that's a vastly different story than the one told by the evolutionists.

Some have suggested that evolutionists and believers in creation can compromise. Is this possible? Could they *both* be right? We'll look at that in the next chapter.

CHAPTER TEN

Searching For Middle Ground
Could God Have Used the Process of Evolution to Create?

Sam Andrews was the man who taught John D. Rockefeller how to refine crude oil with sulfuric acid. He was also major shareholder in the Standard Oil empire. In 1878 Rockefeller decided to issue a fifty percent dividend on the company's stock, a move that upset Andrews—not because he thought the dividend was too high, but because it seemed too small.

He grumbled about the stingy payout for a time, and then one day finally lost his temper with Rockefeller. "I wish I was out of this business!" he said.

John calmly looked him over and said, "Sam, it seems to me that you don't have much faith in the way I'm running this company, and I'm willing to buy you out. How much will you take for your shares?"

"I'll take a million dollars," said Andrews. A million dollars, of course, was an absolute fortune in 1878.

"Give me twenty-four hours to think about it, and we'll talk again in the morning," said Rockefeller. They parted company for the night.

The next morning, when Andrews came to work, Rockefeller presented him with a check for $1 million. He accepted it, happy to get such a good price for his shares. It almost felt like he had taken John to the cleaners.

Rockefeller, however, turned around and immediately sold the shares to William Vanderbilt for $1.3 million. When Sam Andrews found out, his bitterness deepened and he cried foul. Upon hearing this, Rockefeller immediately sent a messenger over to Andrews' home to tell him that he could buy his shares back at the original price but Andrews refused because of his wounded pride.

By 1930, with the Great Depression in full swing, the shares that Andrews had refused to buy for $1 million were worth $900 million. Chances are you don't remember Sam Andrews, and that's because nobody remembers the man who was *almost* one of the richest men in the world.

Bailing out too soon can be a costly mistake. When Darwinism began to sweep through intellectual circles, many Christians struggled with how they could reconcile their biblical faith with the "science" of Darwin's theory. It was clear that the two accounts of human origins were utterly incompatible. Both of them simply could not be true at the same time.

Sir Julian Huxley, a prominent evolutionist, underscored the incompatibility of evolution and the biblical account of creation in his book, *Evolution After Darwin*:

...in the evolutionary pattern of thought there is no longer either need or room for the supernatural. The earth was not created, it evolved. So did all the animals and plants that inhabit it, including our human selves....[48]

The whole point of the theory of evolution—the thing that, in my opinion, breathes life into it—is the obliteration of the supernatural. It is not a new science that has revealed God's true methods of working. It is an attempt to remove God from the picture altogether. Julian Huxley is right: there is no room for God in the theory of evolution.

However, in the face of Darwinism's growing popularity, some Christians pushed aside the issue of incompatibility and started making compromises. It was suggested that perhaps both the creation account and evolution could be true at the same time. What if God created the world through the process of evolution? Wouldn't that make room for everybody?

The urge to compromise is understandable, particularly in light of the intellectual revolution that took place after the close of the Dark Ages. Science replaced theology as the queen of the academic disciplines, and powers of human reason were enthroned on the university campuses of Europe. Much good came from this transition: it yielded, among other things, modern medicine. Superstition was pushed into a closet, and rightly so. However, at the same time, people of faith started to struggle with issues of respectability. If you believed in something that couldn't be tested in a laboratory, you were considered simple.

Nobody wants to be thought of as a simpleton, including Christians. Even though they were adherents of the most reasonable faith in the world, the one that actually gave rise to modern science (after all, the early scientists worked from the principle that there was order, a *plan*, to be discovered in the universe), they scrambled to save their respectability. But like Sam Andrews they sold out far too soon.

The theory that God used evolutionary processes to create the universe is known as *Theistic Evolution*. The six days of creation mentioned in Genesis are explained away as massively long periods of time—perhaps millions of years each. The whole story of creation was turned into a complex allegory for the sake of compatibility with a theory that was in its infancy. The years ahead would prove that Darwinists had far less proof than they originally thought, making the compromise now seem hasty. As Robert Jastrow pointed out for us a little earlier in this book, the scientists now appear to be catching up with the theologians, rather than the other way around.

In the nineteenth and early twentieth centuries it didn't really seem that way. Science was mocking people of faith and shattering their belief systems. Compromise seemed like the way out; it allowed people to be "rational" and Christian at the same time. But biblically speaking, Theistic Evolution runs into several insurmountable problems.

One of the first problems is found in several well-known passages from the New Testament:

Therefore, just as through one man sin entered the world, and death through sin, and thus death spread to all men, because all sinned...
(Romans 5:12)

For if by the one man's offense death reigned through the one, much more those who receive abundance of grace and of the gift of righteousness will reign in life through the One, Jesus Christ. (Romans 5:17)

For the wages of sin is death, but the gift of God is eternal life in Christ Jesus our Lord. (Romans 6:23)

But each one is tempted when he is drawn away by his own desires and enticed. Then, when desire has conceived, it gives birth to sin; and sin, when it is full-grown, brings forth death. (James 1:14, 15)

The Bible is crystal clear in its declaration that *all* death is the result of the human choice to sin. The Genesis account states that even non-human death is the result of our choice to separate ourselves from

God; the whole world, over which we were given dominion, was cursed because of our actions.

This is not a minor concept in Christian theology. Everything hinges on it. We have death through sin, and life through Jesus Christ. Without this concept, the cross becomes a meaningless death, and we have no real explanation for human suffering. If you take away the story of creation as you find it in the book of Genesis, you lose the whole plan of salvation.

Why? It's simple. If God created the world through the process of evolution, using billions of years of a brutal survival-of-the-fittest planet to finally arrive at human civilization, it means that death and suffering occurred millions of times before man even had a *chance* to sin. Death and suffering are no longer the wages of sin, and God created them. It's an idea that defies the entire tone of the Bible, which demonstrates God's purity and innocence, and *our* responsibility for death. The first chapter of Genesis has God declaring His creation "very good," which speaks very poorly of God if death and suffering were already built into the package.

In order to make the compromise between the Bible and the Darwinists, you need to not only allegorize the first two chapters of Genesis, but the entire Bible. Some have attempted to find the line where allegory suddenly becomes historical reality in the timeline of biblical events, but it's a line that is impossible to find because it's not there. The Bible presents its history as fact.

That brings us to our second problem, which is related. Jesus also spoke of the Bible as fact, and He mentioned the Genesis account in particular:

But from the beginning of the creation, God "made them male and female." "For this reason a man shall leave his father and mother and be joined to his wife, and the two shall become one flesh"; so then they are no longer two, but one flesh. Therefore what God has joined together, let not man separate.
(Mark 10:6, 7)

Jesus, the faultless Son of God, apparently believed the creation story, stating in John 10:35 that "scripture cannot be broken." He explained to the Pharisees that marriage was an institution created by God Himself in the Garden of Eden, and there is not the slightest hint in His statement to suggest that He believed the story to be mythological or allegorical. (If anybody knows what really happened at creation, it would be Jesus. In several places, the Bible declares Him to be the Creator—see John 1, Colossians 1, and Hebrews 1.)

There are three conclusions we can come to:

- Jesus didn't know any better. (Not likely, given that He is named as the Creator.)
- Jesus was deliberately misleading people. (Also not likely, given that Jesus was never shy about making statements that ran contrary to popular belief, and given that the Bible states He had "no deceit in His mouth" and He was sinless.[49])
- Jesus was telling the truth.

The writers of the New Testament also make reference to the creation account and man's rebellion as the origin of human suffering as if they are fact. Some might be tempted to argue that the New Testament writers simply hadn't seen the fossil record and didn't know any better, but that assumption runs up against plain statements that declare scripture to be inspired by God:

And so we have the prophetic word confirmed, which you do well to heed as a light that shines in a dark place, until the day dawns and the morning star rises in your hearts; knowing this first, that no prophecy of Scripture is of any private interpretation, for prophecy never came by the will of man, but holy men of God spoke as they were moved by the Holy Spirit. (2 Peter 1:19-21)

All Scripture is given by inspiration of God, and is profitable for doctrine, for reproof, for correction, for instruction in righteousness, that the man of God may be complete, thoroughly equipped for every good work.
(2 Timothy 3:16, 17)

If we allegorize the book of Genesis, or the first few chapters of it, we run into a massive problem: the cohesiveness and authenticity of the entire Bible is severely compromised. It becomes nothing but a cultural and historical document, an object of study for a university literature class and little more. Evolutionists have been stating this for years. It turns out they've been more honest than some Christians who want to compromise where compromise is not possible without undermining the very foundations of the faith.

There is another major point of incompatibility between Darwin and the authors of the Bible. The theory of evolution points to a constant progression of life, with each new generation improving on the one that came before it. The Bible tells a different story, however: one of regression. With the passage of time, suffering and wickedness grow worse, not better.

The creators of the second *Star Trek* series unwittingly emphasize this point. The crew of the starship Enterprise are an advanced civilization that occasionally bumps up against less developed cultures. They refuse to make contact with pre-technological planets so as not to interfere with their natural evolutionary development. They don't want to be mistaken for gods and have some unfortunate civilization inadvertently pushed into the Dark Ages because they became religious.

The idea is, of course, that as evolution progresses, the human race will not only advance technologically, but they will also become ethically superior, having shaken off the shackles of religion. Life is assumed to be *better* in the future, simply because of evolution.

The writers of *Star Trek* appear to have ignored some key facts, not the least of which is the moral degradation our world underwent after it lost its grip on faith. Nietzsche, realizing how the world would change as it let go of faith, predicted that the twentieth century would be the bloodiest in human history. He was absolutely right. With God out of the picture, moral restraint disappeared, and our world has been sliding downhill ever since.

Evolution paints a rosy future picture of human morality. The Bible tells a completely different story:

But know this, that in the last days perilous times will come: For men will be lovers of themselves, lovers of money, boasters, proud, blasphemers, disobedient to parents, unthankful, unholy, unloving, unforgiving, slanderers, without self-control, brutal, despisers of good, traitors, headstrong, haughty, lovers of pleasure rather than lovers of God, having a form of godliness but denying its power. And from such people turn away! (2 Timothy 3:1-5)

Almost every human attempt to predict the future of our planet has failed. Marx predicted class struggles and revolution would lead to relative utopia (an idea tied closely to Darwinism). He was wrong. The Apostle Paul hit the nail right on the head.

The Bible doesn't show the world gradually heading for utopia; it shows God pushing the *restart* button because things eventually move beyond the point of no return. Jesus referred to the events surrounding the flood as an predictor of what would happen in the final moments of Earth's history. Jude points us to Sodom and Gomorrah, and Peter declares that God wipes out this tainted world to give us a new one that is built from scratch:

But the day of the Lord will come as a thief in the night, in which the heavens will pass away with a great noise, and the elements will melt with fervent heat; both the earth and the works that are in it will be burned up. Therefore, since all these things will be dissolved, what manner of persons ought you to be in holy conduct and godliness, looking for and hastening the coming of the day of God, because of which the heavens will be dissolved, being on fire, and the elements will melt with fervent heat? Nevertheless we, according to His promise, look for new heavens and a new earth in which righteousness dwells. (2 Peter 3:10-12)

Other passages make the same promise:

Now I saw a new heaven and a new earth, for the first heaven and the first earth had passed away. Also there was no more sea. Then I, John, saw the holy city, New Jerusalem, coming down out of heaven from God, prepared as a bride adorned for her husband. And I heard a loud voice from heaven saying, "Behold, the tabernacle of God is with men, and He will dwell with them, and they shall be His people. God Himself will be with them and be their God. And God will wipe away every tear from their eyes; there shall be no more death, nor sorrow, nor crying. There shall be no more pain, for the former things have passed away." (Revelation 21:1-4)

"For behold, I create new heavens and a new earth; and the former shall not be remembered or come to mind. But be glad and rejoice forever in what I create; for behold, I create Jerusalem as a rejoicing, and her people a joy. I will rejoice in Jerusalem, and joy in My people; the voice of weeping shall no longer be heard in her, nor the voice of crying. (Isaiah 65:17-19)

The stories are incompatible. The Bible begins with Paradise, moves to ruin and degradation, and holds out the promise that God will intervene and recreate this world back to its original form. Darwin has the world beginning with brutality and suffering, and holds out the promise that we will eventually adapt to our surroundings and things will get better all by themselves.

Something in the human heart is profoundly uncomfortable with the Darwinian understanding. It's not a coincidence that Darwinists are finding evolution a tough sell in the Western World, even after a century and a half of chipping away at the faith community. The vast majority still chooses to believe in a Creator God because it explains our existence so much better than evolution. Our instincts can see past the illusion that things are getting better all by themselves. Our hearts are restless because we don't see improvement. We know things are getting worse. We can't find hope.

A little while ago, a friend of mine loaned me a book. As I thumbed through it, I stumbled across a couple of statements made by a young man looking for the meaning of life which quite nicely sum up the inadequacy of science to explain the human situation:

If I do lose faith, that is if I do let go of my metaphysical explanations for the human experience, it will not be at the hands of science. I went to a Stephen Hawking lecture not long ago and wondered about why he thought we get born and why we die and what it means, but I left with nothing, save a brief mention of aliens as a possible solution to the question of origin. And I don't mean anything against Stephen Hawking, because I know he has an amazing brain and I know he has explained a lot of the physics of our universe, but I went wondering about something scientific that might counter mysterious metaphysical explanations and I left with aliens.[50]

It turns out that the droplet of our knowledge is a bit lost in the ocean of our unknowing. So much so we are still stabbing at fairy tales. And what I really mean by this is science itself is not capable of presenting a why. That is, in order to subscribe to a why, (an objective rather than a subjective why), you have to subscribe to some sort of theory about God or aliens. And yet the mind needs a why, just as the body needs food.[51]

The so-called evidence for the theory of evolution is disappearing. It turns out the two theories are incompatible because evolution simply isn't true. Those who choose to cling to the Bible record, however, are finding rich dividends as science now scrambles to catch up with the wisdom God imparted to us thousands of years ago. We exist for a reason. God made us with a purpose.

In the Canadian Arctic, the Inuit use *inukshuks* as direction finders in places where there are no natural landmarks. An inukshuk is a pile of stones, usually shaped like a man with legs, arms, and a head. It is made in the image of the person who built it, and is left behind by travelers to point the way to their settlement, the nearest village, or some other important place. A while ago I was discussing inukshuks with an Inuit friend who told me, "If you're going to build an inukshuk, you'd better have a purpose for it." You don't just build them for fun. They *all* have a purpose.

The Bible declares that God created us in His image. And like the inukshuk, we were not created "just for fun." We were created with a purpose. Even to this day, our hearts fail to shut out the voice of our Creator altogether. We know there *must* be a purpose to life. Evolution provides us none. It fails to address some of the most essential questions of human existence. It is not an answer; not for origins, and not for purpose. It tells us we are meaningless, when our experience suggests that can't be true. Perhaps, more than any other reason, this is why evolution is so profoundly at odds with the message of the Bible.

Maybe we sold out too soon. Buy your shares back as quickly as you can.

CHAPTER ELEVEN

Arguments Against the Existence of God
Number Six: The "Facts" of the Fossil record

I wasn't very old when I first realized that the ground was full of animal remains, and that some of them were animals that didn't look much like anything you could find at the zoo. Once I figured out that many sedimentary rocks had fossils inside, I went on a rock-splitting binge that yielded quite a few specimens, some of which I donated to the museum in Smithers, my hometown. (They weren't very good fossils, but the curator of the small museum took pity on me and put a couple of them on display for a few weeks.)

A naturalist once told a group of us kids that the fossil beds took millions of years to form, and each successive layer of earth held clues as to the evolutionary history of planet Earth. The simplest life forms were to be found on the bottom layers, he explained, and the most complex were at the top. It seemed logical enough at the time, even though I had not been raised with the theory of evolution.

Those fossil layers have been used all over the world to help date the various things we find in the earth, the assumption being that the layers are pretty much uniform all over the planet. So if you find something in the top layers, it is assumed to be of relatively recent origin; if you find it at the bottom, you can assume it is ancient. There are scientific names given to each layer of sediment, each of which represents a different stage of Earth's history. For the purpose of this discussion, it's not important which layer represents which epoch in history. I only want to ask one question: is the gradual deposit of layers over millions of years the *only* explanation for this phenomenon?

You'd think so, the way most high school textbooks read. The evolutionary timeline, as presented in the fossil record, is pretty much presented as fact. But there are lots of unanswered questions that never seem to make it into most educational diagrams.

For example, take the stunning lack of transitional life forms. If the theory of evolution is a scientific fact, as the Darwinian establishment loves to emphasize, there should be lots of examples of gradual transition from one life form to another; such as a number of successive animals that clearly demonstrate the gradual development from fish to reptile. There are, after all, a *lot* of fossils in the ground. Yet such life forms are problematically absent—so much so that evolutionists have had to develop things like the theory of *punctuated equilibrium* to explain why we can't find any clear transitions.

Punctuated equilibrium says that evolution moves forward in sudden (and dramatic) fits and starts, kind of like a new driver in a standard shift car jerking in and out of gear. It is said that new life forms suddenly appear in large numbers, and then the process of evolution pops back out of gear for millions of years. It's a theory that's not very intellectually satisfying, and there is almost no evidence to support it.

Sometimes evolutionists will pull out *Archaeopteryx* as decisive proof that the fossil record contains transitional life forms. *Archaeopteryx* is said to be a reptile on its way to becoming a bird; a lizard with feathers and wings, if you will. People have been debating this fossil for well over a century, and its identity is far from established. Exactly what *Archaeopteryx* was is still a matter of debate, and some have even questioned whether or not the feather imprints were added to the remains later. At the very least, we know that evolutionists cannot claim *Archaeopteryx* as a transition between reptile and bird and maintain their insistence that the geological strata were laid down over immense periods of time, because fully developed birds have been discovered in layers much deeper than the ones *Archaeopteryx* was discovered in. In other words, there were already birds in the sky before *Archaeopteryx* supposedly became a transition between reptiles and birds!

Before we move on from the subject of transitional life forms, let me make one other quick point. As I was crossing a bridge in Budapest a while ago, admiring the stunning beauty of that city, a thought suddenly crossed my mind. If we really descended from lower animals, why is it that the human race stands so far apart from the rest of the animal kingdom? Why is it that only *our* species builds cities, fills them with beautiful art, and surfs the Internet on cell phones? If all life is progressing along the mystical timeline of evolution, why are there no other animals that have made any advancement at all? Where are the monkeys, for example, that have begun to fashion knives and put axles through wheels?

The gap in achievement between human beings and the rest of the animal kingdom is massive. To suggest that we are like the animals is to ignore the obvious. We may have two eyes like a horse, two legs like a bird, and two arms like a monkey—but we are more dissimilar than evolutionists would care to admit. Some have suggested that termites build houses like we do, but a termite mound is hardly Buckingham Palace. Others have pointed out that chimpanzees and dolphins can learn simple vocabularies of a few hundred symbols, but we have yet to see an animal compose a poem or write a song about the meaning of love. The gap between human and animal is gargantuan compared to the gaps in achievement between the different species of animals.

If all life is transitioning gradually toward higher life forms, then why is the advancement so uneven? Why have other species not developed simple technologies? Evolutionists are at a loss to explain our favored status. But the Bible makes it clear: we were created in the image of God. (And it provided that answer thousands of years before we started asking the question.)

There are other problems with using the fossil record as a uniform measuring stick for the development of life on Earth. There is a great deal of evidence to suggest that dramatic changes on planet Earth (the extinction of species, notable changes in geology, etc.) have not been gradual. They have been the result of catastrophic events.

Consider the abundant mammoth remains found all over the Arctic region. There are islands in the Arctic that boast literally tens of thousands of remains, proving that a species of elephant once roamed the northern region of the planet. In quite a few cases mammoths are not found as fossils, but as frozen carcasses. Some of them still have meat on the bones. We can identify the plants in their stomachs, and according to a few accounts (this has been challenged by some people), some are found with half-chewed food still in their mouths. Zoologist Ivan Sanderson describes one mammoth that appears to have been flash-frozen:

First, the mammoth was upright, but it had a broken hip. Second, its exterior was whole and perfect, with none of its shaggy fur rubbed or torn off. Third, it was fresh; its parts, although they started to rot when the heat of fire got at them, were just as they had been in life; the stomach contents had not begun to decompose. Finally, there were buttercups on its tongue.[52]

Evolutionists are at a loss to explain how in the world millions of mammoths could suddenly be flash-frozen. The catastrophic events surrounding the flood would have created drastic and sudden climate change on an apocalyptic scale (there's a reason Jesus uses the flood in Matthew 24 to describe conditions at the end of the world), and that certainly seems to provide a much better explanation for what we actually find. I mean, just how fast *would* the temperature have to drop in order to freeze a living elephant?

Speaking of the same mammoth, Joseph Dillow makes this observation:

The mammoth must have been overwhelmed suddenly with a rapid deep freeze and instant death. The sudden death is proved by the unchewed bean pods still containing the beans that were found between its teeth, and the deep freeze suggested by the well-preserved state of the stomach contents and the presence of edible meat.... The animal was peacefully grazing in late July, and suddenly within a half hour of ingestion of his last lunch he was overcome by temperatures colder than -150 degrees F, and froze to death in the middle of the summer. Furthermore, he never completely thawed out until he fell out of a river bank in 1901.[53]

The polar regions of the planet were much warmer at one time, providing food for millions of very large animals. Remains of coral reefs have been found in the Canadian Arctic. Fig trees and magnolias have been discovered in Greenland. Plant remains have been found within a few hundred miles of the South Pole.[54]

At some point in the past, the earth underwent drastic changes, and it happened *very quickly*. Millions of years were not needed to catastrophically alter the Arctic into the frozen wasteland that it is today. It happened overnight. The evidence shows it may have taken a matter of *hours*. Perhaps we need to rethink our millions-of-years-for-change model.

We've been told that the oil deposits in the earth took millions of years to form as simple organisms were buried under successive layers of sediment. But researchers have produced oil in a matter of *minutes* in the laboratory, proving that massive time periods are not necessary to make it happen—only heat and pressure:

It has now been demonstrated that cellulosic (plant derived material) such as garbage or manure, can be converted into a good grade of petroleum in twenty minutes.... The experiments of Bureau of Mines scientists in which cow manure was converted to petroleum are described in Chemical and Engineering News, *May 29, 1972, p. 14. The process could also utilize other cellulosic materials such as wood, bark.... The manure was heated at 716 F, at 2000 to 5000 pounds per square inch for twenty minutes in the presence of carbon monoxide and steam. The product was a heavy oil of excellent heating quality. The yield was about three barrels of oil per ton of manure.*[55]

Apparently, you don't need millions of years for oil. Nor do you need millions of years for coal—it's been discovered that we can produce coal in a matter of hours. Furthermore, nowhere in the world today can we find peat (or other organic materials) being transformed into coal by natural processes. If it happened gradually over millions of years, shouldn't we be able to find coal deposits being formed now? The answer is "no," not if the coal in the ground is the result of sudden and catastrophic changes to the planet.

Also consider the way that animals are found in the fossil record. Why is it that millions of animals seem to have died at exactly the same time, with many of them found lying in the same direction? That doesn't happen today. You won't find thousands—or millions—of caribou remains in one spot, all patiently waiting to be covered by sediment. Their remains weather and decompose over a few short years. Yet, at some time in the ancient past, a *lot* of animals were all covered up at the same time.

And how is it that we find so many dinosaur footprints, often in the same place? Did depressions in the soil brave the elements for hundreds—or thousands—or millions—of years as they slowly turned to stone? Think back to your childhood, however long ago that was. You left footprints *somewhere:* on a beach, in the forest, or on a sand dune. Go back and try to find them now. They're long gone. They didn't survive the elements. Yet thousands upon thousands of dinosaur footprints have survived all over the planet.

Why is it that we find fossilized tree remains that poke up through many layers of sediment? Did those logs really stand at attention for twenty million years, waiting patiently to be buried without rotting?

Not likely. Professor Erich von Fange of Concordia University makes this observation:

Great age is assumed from the successive strata in rocks that are believed to have been laid down very slowly and gradually. This is the heart of uniformitarianism in establishing the dating for the geological column from Precambrian to modern times. This principle, however, is not faring well in geological research. As just one example, the trunk of a tree at Craigleth Quarry in England was found to intersect from ten to twelve successive strata of limestone. It became fossilized without even losing its bark. Presumably the tree and its bark survived patiently for many millions of years as the strata covered it millimeter by millimeter. [56]

It just doesn't take very long to cover trees and petrify them. When Mount St. Helens erupted in 1980, it dropped large portions of its forests into Spirit Lake. At first the logs floated on top of the lake, but gradually, as they became waterlogged, they began to sink to the bottom in an upright position. The result was a "forest" at the bottom of the lake. It looks just like the petrified forests we find at places like Yellowstone National Park. (Another interesting observation discovered in the wake of the Mount St. Helens eruption: sediment can be laid down *very* quickly. Some places were covered with as much as a meter of ash in a matter of minutes.) [57] What would have happened in the wake of a global flood?

One more good question: why do we sometimes find the so-called oldest layers of earth on top, and the so-called newest layers on the *bottom*? Why are the fossils sometimes mixed up—with the oldest ones mixed in or even *above* the so-called newest ones? How did that happen?

There are a lot of questions we could ask. Because this is not primarily a geology textbook, we won't ask them all. Enough people have already written books looking at thousands of anomalies that defy the theory of evolution and the idea that conditions on our planet have been uniform for millions of years. Darwinists, however, seldom mention inconvenient discoveries in public, or allow them to be discussed in classrooms, because they need to keep the theory of evolution intact. There's more at stake than mere science.

At its heart evolution is not science, it is a belief system. It has a religious premise. Philosophers in the nineteenth century declared that God was dead—a figment of our imaginations—and Darwin provided the "scientific" groundwork for a radical departure from biblical faith. Atheists *need* evolution to be true in order to bolster their belief system. It is an attempt to reject God without looking as if they are actually rejecting Him; life choices are made because "science" has proven that the world has no real meaning.

Still, the cry from the human heart for meaning cannot be silenced. For some unfortunate souls it ends in suicide: not knowing the importance of your existence robs you of your will to live. For others it leads to a hollow existence where life is spent "punching the clock." Some turn to alcohol in order to silence the ache in their heart, others to other forms of escapism.

The evolutionary establishment laughs at the story of creation, but geological evidence is mounting that a catastrophe—like the biblical flood—best explains what we find in the earth. A global flood would kill millions of animals, all at once. It would radically change the face of the earth (consider the unbelievable damage that occurs when a mere dam breaks.) It explains why we find marine fossils in unusual places, and the remains of animals that don't usually hang out together (predator and prey) buried together. It even explains the heights of mountains and the depths of valleys.

Some have scoffed at the idea of the flood, pointing out that the amount of water needed to cover Mount Everest simply doesn't exist anywhere on the planet. Or so you'd think. As the current furor over global warming demonstrates, we've come to realize that even a little bit of ice melting at either pole would produce catastrophic results for low-lying coastal areas all over the planet. A little while back, alarm bells were sounded when a 41-square-mile piece of the ice shelf broke off from Ellesmere Island in the Canadian Arctic, and scientists pointed to that event as proof that larger pieces might start breaking off in the near future, which would cause catastrophic flooding and weather changes all over the planet.

As it turns out, according to some estimates there is enough ice right now on the continent of Antarctica to cover the entire planet with a layer of ice about 120 feet thick if it were spread around. (You might want to get out a set of encyclopedias and run your own numbers for the fun of it.) That represents a *lot* of water if it should melt. Of course, that's still not enough to cover Mount Everest, but it's still a *lot* of water.

Even without the polar ice, there is still enough water in the ocean to cover the entire planet. The deepest point in the ocean is almost 36,000 feet deep—nearly seven miles. The highest point—the top of Mount Everest—is about 29,000 feet above sea level. That means there's a difference of more than twelve miles between the highest and lowest points on Earth. If you took all the dry land on Earth and leveled it off, filling in all the deepest parts of the ocean, there would be enough water to cover the whole world with an ocean about a mile and a half deep. Enough water for a global flood? You bet. All you have to do is change the surface of the earth a little bit, and it would happen again.

And amazingly, thousands of years before the debate erupted, God had the forethought to put the solution in the Bible:

> *You set earth on a firm foundation*
> *so that nothing can shake it, ever.*
> *You blanketed earth with ocean,*
> *covered the mountains with deep waters;*
> *Then you roared and the water ran away—*
> *your thunder crash put it to flight.*
> *Mountains pushed up, valleys spread out*
> *in the places you assigned them.*
> *You set boundaries between earth and sea;*
> *never again will earth be flooded.*
> *(Psalm 104:5-9)*

According to the Bible record, Mount Everest didn't always exist. It wasn't there before the flood; it appeared afterwards, when mountains "pushed up" from the earth.

We have evidence that things we find on top of mountains were once at sea level. Lake Titicaca, which borders Peru and Bolivia, now sits more than 12,000 feet above sea level:

Jacques Cousteau photographed remarkable massive stone blocks fitted into a wall under the lake waters. The wall points directly to the city of Tiahuanaco. There are large expanses of terraced hillsides in the area, but today nothing can be grown on them due to the high elevation.

The age of the city is a controversial question. We do know, however, that drawings of an extinct animal, the toxodon, have been found on pottery fragments there. The Andes rose abruptly in historical times when man was already sailing ships. There was a sea harbor in Lake Titicaca. Rings for ship cables on piers are so large that they would be appropriate only for ocean vessels. Yet today the site is 200 miles from the Pacific Ocean and lies at an altitude of 12,500 feet. Traces of seaweed are found at the lake, and Pacific Ocean seashells are still seen in this part of the Andes. Numerous raised beaches may be seen, and the water in the southern portion of the lake is still salty. The lake has a chalky deposit of ancient seaweeds with lime, about six feet thick, which indicates that the ridge where it is found was once an ancient seashore.

Modern geologists say that the present shore of the lake was once immersed in the ocean. Ocean fauna are found in the lake. A salt line appears on the mountains surrounding the lake. Lake Titicaca was formerly an inlet of the Ocean. A rise of about 2.5 miles in elevation sounds wildly implausible, yet technicians of a Western Telegraph ship searching for a lost cable in the Atlantic in 1923 found that the cable had been lifted 2.25 miles during a 25-year period. The ocean floor was and is far more plastic than anyone had realized.[58]

The earth is not as stable as we'd like to think it is. Sudden and dramatic shifts in elevation have been a reality in the past, and changes in topography take place in timeframes much shorter than evolutionists have led us to believe. In 1949, for example, sand from the bottom of the Atlantic Ocean was brought to the surface in a remote location more than 1,000 miles from any shore. The water was more than three miles deep, and yet the sand contained twigs, nuts and bark fragments. Unbelievably, at some unknown point in the past, the ocean floor in this region had been above sea level. Something made it plunge to a distance of more than three miles.[59]

Apparently, the world was a very busy place during and after the flood, geologically speaking. Mountains quickly pushed up from the earth, millions of life forms died suddenly, and judging by the frozen remains of elephants in the north along with the fossils found of cells in the middle of cell division (how in the world did that become fossilized over the course of millions of years?), the global climate suddenly shifted dramatically.

Our Earth was radically altered by a major catastrophe—the sort described in the Bible. It fits. And it fits better than the notion of millions of years of slow sedimentary build-up.

And yet there are those who stubbornly cling to the theory of evolution, because it creates the illusion that they will never have to deal with God. They *need* the theory to be true, and they *need* the Bible to be a fairy tale, so they deliberately shelter themselves from all the facts. Interestingly, the Bible predicted that would be the case, almost two thousand years ago:

For this they willfully forget: that by the word of God the heavens were of old, and the earth standing out of water and in the water, by which the world that then existed perished, being flooded with water. (2 Peter 3:5, 6)

Read that passage again. It's stunning. Grab a Bible and read the whole chapter. Peter wrote it in the context of people laughing at the Second Coming of Christ in the final moments before it actually happens. He says that people are going to *willfully*—deliberately—forget where they came from so they can deliberately forget where they're going. Centuries before the debate between Darwinists and Creationists, Peter predicted it was going to happen. It's not just a matter of origins, he says, it's also a matter of destiny.

There is a direct correlation between the story of creation, the biblical account of the flood, and the Second Coming of Christ. If you write off the creation story as a fable, and scorn the flood as mythology, chances are you won't believe that Christ is returning, either. That, of course, would prove to be a very serious mistake on the day you see Him coming.

CHAPTER TWELVE

Out of Thin Air

Off the coast of Iceland, there's an island that is brand new. And by brand new, I don't mean that somebody recently discovered it and gave it a name. It's literally brand new. A few decades ago the island of Surtsey didn't exist, and then volcanic eruptions made it rise out of the ocean. Presto: a brand new plot of dry land!

Of course, you don't hear much about this island in high school textbooks, because it proves that you don't need much time to make something completely new on planet Earth, even on a large scale. In the space of a few short years, this amazing island had already developed a thriving ecosystem all its own: birds, plant life, the whole bit. But at the same time, we're told it's not possible that an Almighty God brought our world into existence in six short days.

Our present unbelief stems from the biggest problem human beings have: pride. We are a very proud race of beings, absolutely convinced that we are the center of the universe. If we don't understand it, and our instruments can't measure it, it must not be true.

Don't get me wrong. I'm a big fan of science. I find the study of our universe absolutely fascinating. But I have to admit that I really don't get it all. Anybody with human limitations—even if they're hundreds of times more advanced than I am in the disciplines of science (not that difficult an achievement)—will have to admit the same thing. There is simply more information in this universe that we do *not* know than we *do* know.

Centuries ago one of the finest minds in the world, a Greek by the name of Aristotle, sincerely believed that men and women had different numbers of teeth. There was also a time when we believed that fire was caused by a mysterious substance called *phlogiston*. We used to think that atoms were simply made up of protons, neutrons, and electrons. But now we have the means to look more closely, and we've discovered an amazing world even smaller than those well-known particles. Until just recently we were absolutely convinced that Jupiter had twelve moons and that Pluto qualified as a planet in the same way that the other planets in our solar system do.

We had to change our mind about all those things. As science progresses, we will have to change our minds many more times. In the same way that we look back and smile at the simplicity of our forefathers, we should understand that if history continues, one day our descendants will also look back and smile at us.

Our cell phones may seem as inconvenient as smoke signals. Our fancy SUVs may be as antiquated as a horse-drawn carriage. Our current understanding of chemistry and geology and physics will be a source of amusement as families play Trivial Pursuit on a Saturday night a hundred years from now, should Jesus delay His return that long.

So why, in the face of mounting evidence that our theory of evolution was absolutely mistaken, do we stubbornly cling to it? If we were really truthful, would we admit that it's because we don't actually want God in the picture?

Let's be honest—to say with certainty that there is no God, we would have to explore a little more of the universe than the Apollo space program did. Before we rule out the miraculous stories of the Bible, we should probably come to grips with quantum mechanics and the unpredictable behavior of subatomic particles. Maybe before we say that Jesus of Nazareth couldn't possible rise from the dead, we should first figure out exactly how light works.

Erich von Fange makes an amazing point in his book, *In Search of the Genesis World:*

It would be difficult to better illustrate what science ought to be than the contents of an amazing book The Encyclopedia of Ignorance. *Some of the world's leading scientists leaped at the opportunity to contribute chapters on what they did not know about their specialties. As the editor stated, "The more eminent they were, the more ready they were to run to us with their ignorance." Is it any surprise that this remarkable book devotes more space to the problems of evolution, including the supposed evolution of man, and mysteries of astronomy than any other pair of topics? The Big Bang and the supposed vast age of the universe, ape-to-man theory, and evolution itself are so riddled with assumptions, guesswork, and unsupported opinions that we have no actual evidence standing in the way of accepting Genesis just as it reads.*[60]

One of my favorite passages in the Bible is the description of God visiting Job. Job had been asking questions, not the scientific questions that ask *how*, but the bigger questions that start with *why*. Pay careful attention to God's answer:

> *Then the Lord answered Job out of the whirlwind, and said:*
> *"Who is this who darkens counsel*
> *By words without knowledge?*
> *Now prepare yourself like a man;*
> *I will question you, and you shall answer Me.*
> *Where were you when I laid the foundations of the earth?*
> *Tell Me, if you have understanding.*
> *Who determined its measurements?*
> *Surely you know!*
> *Or who stretched the line upon it?*
> *To what were its foundations fastened?*
> *Or who laid its cornerstone,*
> *When the morning stars sang together,*
> *And all the sons of God shouted for joy?*
> *Or who shut in the sea with doors,*
> *When it burst forth and issued from the womb;*
> *When I made the clouds its garment,*
> *And thick darkness its swaddling band;*
> *When I fixed My limit for it,*
> *And set bars and doors;*
> *When I said,*
> *'This far you may come, but no farther,*
> *And here your proud waves must stop!'*
> *Have you commanded the morning since your days began,*
> *And caused the dawn to know its place,*
> *That it might take hold of the ends of the earth,*
> *And the wicked be shaken out of it?*
> *It takes on form like clay under a seal,*
> *And stands out like a garment.*
> *From the wicked their light is withheld,*
> *And the upraised arm is broken.*

Have you entered the springs of the sea?
  Or have you walked in search of the depths?
Have the gates of death been revealed to you?
  Or have you seen the doors of the shadow of death?
Have you comprehended the breadth of the earth?
  Tell Me, if you know all this.
Where is the way to the dwelling of light?
  And darkness, where is its place,
That you may take it to its territory,
  That you may know the paths to its home?
Do you know it, because you were born then,
  Or because the number of your days is great?
Have you entered the treasury of snow,
  Or have you seen the treasury of hail,
Which I have reserved for the time of trouble,
  For the day of battle and war?
By what way is light diffused,
  Or the east wind scattered over the earth?
Who has divided a channel for the overflowing water,
  Or a path for the thunderbolt,
To cause it to rain on a land where there is no one,
  A wilderness in which there is no man;
To satisfy the desolate waste,
  And cause to spring forth the growth of tender grass?
Has the rain a father?
  Or who has begotten the drops of dew?
From whose womb comes the ice?
  And the frost of heaven, who gives it birth?
The waters harden like stone,
  And the surface of the deep is frozen.
Can you bind the cluster of the Pleiades,
  Or loose the belt of Orion?
Can you bring out Mazzaroth in its season?
  Or can you guide the Great Bear with its cubs?
Do you know the ordinances of the heavens?
  Can you set their dominion over the earth?
Can you lift up your voice to the clouds,
  That an abundance of water may cover you?

Can you send out lightnings, that they may go,
  And say to you, 'Here we are!'?
Who has put wisdom in the mind?
  Or who has given understanding to the heart?
Who can number the clouds by wisdom?
  Or who can pour out the bottles of heaven,
When the dust hardens in clumps,
  And the clods cling together?
Can you hunt the prey for the lion,
  Or satisfy the appetite of the young lions,
When they crouch in their dens,
  Or lurk in their lairs to lie in wait?
Who provides food for the raven,
  When its young ones cry to God,
And wander about for lack of food?
(Job 38)

You should probably read through that passage a couple of times before you go on with the rest of this chapter. In fact, you should go hunt down a good Bible and read chapter 39 as well. God asks some really important questions, all of them designed to prove how little we actually know. At the same time, the direct implication is that God *does* know, and the universe is in good hands.

One the most interesting questions God asks is "where is the dwelling place of light?" For the most part, we don't even know exactly what light is. Is it made of particles, or is it a wave? Is it possible that it's made of both? We may be able to produce, manipulate and measure light, but we really don't understand a lot about it. And if light didn't already exist, we would be incapable of producing it, because all of our inventions essentially mimic something we find in nature. We are creative, but we are not creators. We cannot develop a brand new concept out of thin air—something that nobody has ever seen before. We might as well try to imagine a brand new primary color. It simply can't be done.

And that's God's point. He *does* know how to do those things. You'll notice that the list of things we still don't understand is pretty long in that chapter. We might have theories about some of God's points. We might have learned to measure some of them. But we don't really know how or why they came into being, apart from what the Creator has told us.

Job's issue was undue suffering, one of the things still raised by atheists today as proof that God must not exist. All through the book he and his friends discuss important philosophical questions, but at the end of the day, they didn't have the answers they wanted. So God shows up and asks the big questions Himself. And to be perfectly honest and fair in the debate between creation and evolution, we should submit ourselves to some of the more pertinent themes in God's line of questioning:

• Were we there when God created the heavens and the Earth? Can we measure the question of origins on a strictly scientific basis when we didn't see the process happen the first time, and we find ourselves incapable of granting life to even primitive forms of life?

• How is it that simple things—like the march of the planets around our sun and the demarcation between sea and land—make this planet such a perfect place for us to live? We assume that, statistically speaking, there are many other planets like us in the cosmos, but we have never seen them.

• Do we really know, strictly through observance of phenomena, what's on the other side of the grave? (I need to write a book on this one—the Bible reveals a startling picture.)

• How do you give birth to something as complex as light? The Bible says God spoke it into existence—out of thin air—but we have yet to fully understand it, let alone create something as complex as light.

• We might be able to predict weather (with a rather large margin of error), but how do you produce weather or alter it?

• Why are there entire ecosystems on Earth that human eyes never lay eyes on? Are those strictly for God's enjoyment? Is He waiting for us to discover them? (This thought was prompted by the question about rain falling in the wilderness where there is no man.)

The point of God's soliloquy is abundantly clear: when it comes right down to it, human beings don't know very much. So to pronounce with any degree of certainty that the creation story is not possible, and that our theory of evolution is a superior (and more intelligent) explanation is the height of arrogance. Particularly when the weight of the evidence seems to fall on the side of the Bible accounts of creation and the deluge.

As the Dark Ages came to a close, we began to believe that everything could be understood and every problem solved through the power of man's intellect. On the one hand, it was a positive development: God expects us to use our powers of reason. He invites us to discover the universe He created and marvel at His design. But on the other hand, to suggest that our intellect has no limits is dangerous thinking. We have had to repent of our opinions and decisions many times already. Our decision to give up on God gave us the Second World War and unspeakable atrocities. It has given us broken families, a high prevalence of sexually transmitted diseases, high crime rates, and a whole lot of other social maladies.

The tragic part of the decline of Western civilization is that it is based on a theory that literally comes out of thin air. There is no real support for Darwinism. The transitional life forms that would prove the theory are missing. The fossil record speaks of massive catastrophic events rather than millions of gradual years of change. The processes we have been told that led to the development of species seem to be absent from nature today. The only mutations we have witnessed are negative ones that impair function rather than improve it. And there is still a nagging desire in our lives to discover the meaning of life.

If Darwin is right, why do we crave meaning? Who gave us that desire? What purpose could the evolution of our self-awareness and desire for importance serve? The theory doesn't make sense. It doesn't answer our biggest questions. But the Bible, which says that God created this world out of nothing at all—out of thin air, if you will—answers the questions. It makes sense. And that's why so many of us can't shake the idea of God. He's real, and He's been telling us the truth all along.

EPILOGUE

Iceland is a geological wonder, the kind of place everyone should see at least once in his or her life. The surface is covered with spectacular lava flows. Green fields of jagged volcanic rock are full of piping hot geysers. Breathtaking waterfalls, glaciers and rivers dot the countryside. To visit Iceland is to almost step back into a time when most of the planet was wilderness.

A little while ago I went swimming with some friends in Iceland at eleven o'clock at night. The outdoor pool was located behind the facility where we were speaking at a European youth convention, and the pool was heated with geothermal water. You could see spouts of steam coming out of the ground everywhere.

We were hoping to see the northern lights, and we did. It wasn't an overly spectacular display, but it was still very beautiful. And as we were *oohing* and *aahing* over the dancing drapes of faded green spectral light, I couldn't help but wonder: why do we love this so much? Why is it so compelling? Why do we love beauty?

How in the world could the theory of evolution explain the sheer ecstasy we feel when we hear a Brahms concerto? Why do I pause by a Salvador Dali painting to sit down and soak it in? Why does a poem by Lord Byron suddenly arrest my attention—even though I don't generally enjoy poetry—as I notice how brilliantly it's been constructed? Why are flowers so beautiful? Why does the isolation of sitting on the peak of a mountain I've just climbed—where the piercing wind draws tears of protest from my eyes—do more than simply imprint a visual image of the scenery on my brain? Why does it also move me deeply in my heart and soul?

Evolutionists must fall silent on these issues. There have been paltry attempts to explain the wonderful emotions that go with things like art and music, but the explanations seem a little forced and don't really do much to satisfy those who find sheer joy in the beautiful.

And have you ever noticed that somehow standing in front of a lofty mountain or beautiful river running through a forest can enrapture you with its beauty, even though everything you see is asymmetrical, with a order that is not immediately apparent to the human eye? When *we* create things of beauty, it has a much simpler order to it. We like neat things: squares, ellipses, curves, and the like. But nature doesn't quite do it that way. It's much more complex, vastly less obvious, and yet it's more beautiful to look at than anything else *we* have managed to create.

Have you ever wondered why you can stare into the water for hours on end and never get tired of it, or why you can sit perched on a mountaintop for hours, ogling the vista, hoping that it doesn't get dark for a long time so you look a little longer? How in the world would an evolutionist explain *that*? If you were staring at the forest because you were worried about predators lurking among the trees, that would fit into the plan of evolution. If you were watching the river to see where the fish were jumping so you could catch your dinner, that could also be woven into a theory of evolution. That makes sense. But to just stare at the forest for *fun*? What evolutionary purpose does that serve?

Don't forget, staring at the beautiful is a nigh-universal human trait. Most of us do it. We might have varying tastes in beauty, but we all have things that arrest our attention and make us look again. Staring at something in sheer appreciation of aesthetic beauty doesn't serve any function whatsoever in the survival-of-the-fittest motif. And yet, because it *is* so universal, for Darwinism to be true, it must have evolved at some point. Why? It doesn't make sense.

If you consider the creation account, it makes perfect sense. According to the book of Genesis, God stood back at the end of creation week, looked over what He had made, and said, "it is *very* good." God is a Creator. He loves to be creative—and He loves to appreciate good things. The Bible says we were made in His image. We have a desire to create. We take joy in drawing a good picture or planting a beautiful flower garden. We derive pleasure from inventing new ways of doing things, and we love to exercise the creative privilege God granted us in making it possible for us to have offspring.

A God who loves those things made us creative, fun loving, and artistic. Evolution couldn't possibly make that happen. Scientists search the brain, trying to figure out why we laugh and how we determine whether or not something's funny. They're missing the point. Chemical processes clearly take place in the brain when we're laughing, but instinctively we know that laughter is more than just a chemical reaction. We are not mere machines. We laugh because we are *human*, and that means something. Hyenas and chimps and some birds can laugh, but it's not the same thing. None of them told a joke. None of them saw the irony in a statement made by another animal. That's a *human* quality.

We know how to love, how to empathize or sympathize, and how to put ourselves in another perspective in order to analyze a situation. Not only can I think about a situation and think through the consequences years into the future, I can mentally put myself in *your* shoes, look at it from *your* perspective and do the same thing. I know of no animal that can do that. Crows and parrots can mimic our sounds. Monkeys can mimic our actions. But they can't perform the exercise of mentally jumping inside your head and watching the world from your perspective.

We are different from the animals in a thousand different ways. And there are *billions* of us. If you're a computer user, download Google Earth (it's a free program) and take a look at our planet from outer space. Zoom in and allow the planet to slowly rotate at an elevation where you can make out various cities—at least the large ones. Then grab the globe and give it a gentle spin, so that the ground starts rolling by slowly. Take an hour or two to sit and watch it—I promise you it's worth the time. Watch the masses of people go by. Watch the splendor of the Himalayan mountains pass before you in startling detail. Trace over the vast expanse of Arctic snow and rock. And then ask yourself: *does this really mean nothing?*

Is planet Earth just a big ant pile for humans, who are doomed to perform routine tasks for an invisible queen ant every day of our insignificant lives until it's time to punch out? Is that all there is? Does it really mean nothing?

If you have children, take them to the beach or stream and watch them play. Why do they find everything from twigs to bugs fascinating? Why do they stuff their pockets full of rocks and cry when you tell them they can't take a rotting tree branch home in the back of the car? Why do they chase a grasshopper for miles?

It's human curiosity. We're determined, from the very earliest stages of life, to figure out what this place is all about. We want to know how stuff works. That's what made us scientists. But we also want to know what stuff means. And that's the bigger question. It makes all of us philosophers and theologians. Instinctively, we know there's a reason that things work. We know there's a *how*. But just as instinctively, we know there's a *why*, too.

We don't just want to know *how* we got here—evolution has created a myth that can be used to answer that question—we want to know *why*. And the Bible answers both questions.

As we watched the northern lights from the pool, those who had never seen them were asking *how* it happens. What causes it? Then somebody made a joke about how the Icelandic government pays a man with a powerful flashlight to stand just over the hill and wave it about. We laughed. Then it occurred to me: that's exactly what the evolutionists are doing. They're running out of actual evidence, so they spend a lot of time sending people out with flashlights to make us think there's really something going on.

The theory of evolution is a man with a flashlight, fooling us into thinking there are northern lights in the sky. They're propping up a faltering theory with a light show. They don't show us all the evidence anymore, because it points in a direction they're afraid of. They're trying to hide the fact that the theory of evolution was pulled out of thin air. It has no support. It rests on hypotheses that require that significant portions of the evidence be ignored. At least in the past, evolutionists were honest enough to point out the holes in their theory. As the number of holes increased, the honesty of the evolutionists seems to have evaporated. They speak of evolution as a fact, when it is far from having been proved. We are still waiting for evidence, and nobody seems to be able to point to any.

On the other hand, the story of creation has real answers. It explains our world. It explains the desires of our hearts. It explains the stuff we find in the ground. There's no man on the horizon with a flashlight trying to fool us with a half-baked theory. Just honest-to-goodness northern lights, a creation spoken into existence by the voice of God. God spoke, and the world came into being—right out of thin air.

ENDNOTES

[1] Joe White et al., Darwin's Demise,
(Green Forest, AR: Master Books, 2001), p. 137.
[2] Ibid., p. 139.
[3] U.S. News and World Report, *Who's Your Daddy?*,
Betsy Streisand, February 13, 2006.
[4] Albert Camus, The Myth of Sysiphus, (New York: Vintage Books, 1991), p. 4.
[5] Viktor Frankl, Man's Search for Meaning, (Boston: Beacon Press, 2006)
[6] Ibid.
[7] Friedrich Nietschze, The Gay Science.
(Mineola, NY: Dover Publications, 2006)
[8] Ibid.
[9] Some will argue a third possibility: there is no evidence. The evidence
presented in this book will demonstrate why I chose to leave this possibility out
of the discussion at this point.
[10] www.geocities.com/missus_gumby/somemore.htm
[11] www.atheistalliance.org/library/nelson-why_atheists.php
[12] It should be noted that those who persecuted John for his religious
convictions were not Christians. Someone might construct a convincing case
that they were motivated by religion nonetheless, since the Roman Empire
officially endorsed freedom of religion, but could not extend full tolerance
to Christians because they were unwilling to add the worship of Caesar to
their religious beliefs. Others might argue that the Romans were inspired
to persecute Christians for political reasons, using religion as an excuse to
eliminate a group perceived to be a threat to the stability of the empire. Either
way, the pagan Roman Empire still exhibited some of the hazards of mixing
church and state by turning its political wrath against Christians on matters of
conscience.
[13] The first two chapters of the book of Romans, for example, make a striking
point. As Paul demonstrates the faults of the Gentiles, he is setting a trap for
believers, pointing out that they do the same things (and worse) and are—
because they have the scriptures—more guilty than their pagan neighbors.
[14] Richard Dawkins, The God Delusion
(New York: Houghton Mifflin Company, 2006), p. 278.
[15] Sergei Kourdakov, The Persecutor,
(Old Tappan, NJ: Fleming H. Revell, 1973), p. 123.
[16] Benjamin Spock, Baby and Child Care, 1957, p. 223.
[17] Modern biology has now rejected the theory in its original form, having
adapted it somewhat to fit their observations. Among other things, it is now
argued that even though humans share common ancestors with other forms of
life, our various stages of fetal development do not resemble the adult versions
of those other life forms. It is now admitted that you cannot pick out "fish" and
"mammal" stages of development. Although the original theory is now

ENDNOTES

considered erroneous and outdated, it did have tremendous impact on 19th century thinking.

[18] Russell Grigg, Ernst Haeckel: Evangelist for Evolution and Apostle of Deceit. Posted at: www.answersingenesis.org/creation/v18/i2/haeckel.asp

[19] Walter J. Bock, "Evolution by Orderly Law," Science, Vol. 164, May 9, 1969, pp. 684-685.

[20] Robert J. Lifton, The Nazi Doctors: Medical Killing and the Psychology of Genocide (New York: Harper Colins Basic Books, 1986), p. 125.

[21] Phil Orenstein, Heil Professor, July 2006. Posted at: www.discoverthenetworks.org/Articles/heilprofessor.html

[22] Richard Dawkins, The God Delusion, p. 273.

[23] Ibid., p. 274.

[24] Ibid.

[25] All three quotes in Dawkins, The God Delusion, p. 276.

[26] Ibid., p. 277.

[27] Ibid., p. 18.

[28] Quoted in Cornelius Hunter, Darwin's God (Brazos Press: 2004), p. 153.

[29] A good example would be Rahab the harlot (Judges 2), who became a progenitor to Christ Himself. (Matthew 1:5)

[30] As happened in 2006 at the memorial service for the victims of the Sago Mine disaster.

[31] I almost hesitate to mention this book because of some of the unwarranted conclusions its author makes about certain Christian groups and their beliefs. Overall, however, the book is useful.

[32] Don Richardson, Eternity in Their Hearts (Ventura, CA: Regal Books, 1984), p. 84.

[33] Ibid., p. 42

[34] Ibid.

[35] Dawkins, p. 114

[36] In Robert Jastrow, God and the Astronomers (New York: W.W. Norton, 1978), p. 116.

[37] Jim Holt, The Wall Street Journal, December 24, 1997.

[38] Stephen C. Meyer, The Explanatory Power of Design, in William A. Dembski, ed., Mere Creation: Science, Faith and Intelligent Design (Downer's Grove, Illinois: InterVarsity Press, 1998), p. 118.

[39] Ibid.

[40] Robert Jastrow, God and the Astronomers (New York: W. W. Norton, 1978), p. 114.

[41] I have lost the original reference for this book, since I have drawn it from a much earlier manuscript I wrote on the origins of man. The book should not be hard to find, however.

[42] mtDNA is more abundant than DNA, and is only passed on by the mother,

E N D N O T E S

which means that variations are caused by mutations rather than the merging of both parents' genes. It is believed that this gives a more accurate history of a species' evolution.

[43] DNA Shows Neandertals Were Not Our Ancestors,
Penn State News Release, 7-11-97.
[44] Burt Thompson, Ph.D., Neanderthal Man–Another Look
(Apologetics Press: May 2002 - 1[5]:17-R-19-R)
[45] John Reader, New Scientist Magazine, March 26, 1981.
[46] A. H. Clark, The New Evolution—Zoogenesis, p. 211.
[47] Ibid., p. 114.
[48] Feyerabend, et al, p. 42.
[49] See 1 Peter 1:22
[50] Donald Miller, Through Painted Deserts
(Nashville: Nelson Books, 2005), p. 25.
[51] Ibid., p. 26.
[52] Ivan T. Anderson, Riddle of the Frozen Giants, quoted in John C.
Whitcomb, the World that Perished (Grand Rapids: Baker, 1991), p. 77.
[53] Joseph Dillow, in Whitcomb, p. 80.
[54] Erich Von Fange, p. 232.
[55] Duane Gish, in Whitcomb, p. 124.
[56] Erich Von Fange, In Search of the Genesis World, p. 223.
[57] Whitbcomb, p. 103.
[58] Erich Von Fange, p. 219.
[59] Ibid., p. 232.
[60] Ibid., p. 338.

BIBLIOGRAPHY

Camus, Albert. *The Myth of Sisyphus and Other Essays.*
New York: Vintage Books. 1991.

Dawkins, Richard. *The God Delusion.*
New York: Houghton Mifflin Company. 2006.

Feyerabend, Henry, and Shawn Boonstra. *Parade of the Pretenders.*
Oshawa, Ontario: It Is Written. 1998.

Ferguson, Kitty. *Stephen Hawking: Quest for a Theory of Everything.*
New York: Bantam Books. 1992.

Frankl, Viktor. *Man's Search for Meaning.* Boston: Beacon Press. 2006.

Hanegraaff, Hank. *The Face That Demonstrates the Farce of Evolution.*
Nashville: Word Publishing. 1998.

Hauser, Marc. *Moral Minds: How Nature Designed Our Universal Sense of Right and Wrong.* New York: Harper Collins. 2006.

Hitler, Adolph. *Mein Kampf.* Boston: Houghton Mifflin Company. 1971.

Jastrow, Robert. *God and the Astronomers.*
New York: W. W. Norton & Company. 1992.

Kourdakov, Sergei. *The Persecutor.* Old Tappan,
New Jersey: Fleming H. Revell Company. 1973.

Miller, Donald. *Through Painted Deserts.* Nashville: Nelson Books. 2005.

Nietzsche, Friedrich. *The Gay Science.*
Mineola, NY: Dover Publications. 2006.

Orenstein, Phil. *Heil Professor!* 2006. Article posted at
www.discoverthenetwork.org/Articles/heilprofessor.html

Richardson, Don. *Eternity in Their Hearts.*
Ventura, CA: Regal Books. 1984.

Roth, Ariel. *Origins: Linking Science and Scripture.*
Hagerstown, MD: Review and Herald Publishing Association. 1998.

Schroeder, Gerald L. *The Hidden Face of God.*
New York: Simon and Schuster. 2001.

von Fange, Erich. *In Search of the Genesis World.*
St. Louis: Concordia Publishing House. 2006.

Wells, Spencer. *Deep Ancestry: Inside the Genographic Project.*
Washington, DC: National Geographic Society. 2006.

Whitcomb, John C. *The World That Perished.*
Grand Rapids: Baker Book House. 1991.

White, Joe and Nicholas Comninellis. *Darwin's Demise.*
Green Forest, AR: Master Books. 2001.

Discover Anwers
to life's
Questions

Bibleinfo.com offers answers to hundreds of everyday questions. Discover what the Bible has to say about your question. The answer is only a click away!

Plus, there is a fun, educational and inspirational site designed for children. Explore interactive games, Bible lessons, character-building stories and more at www.KidsBibleinfo.com.

Bibleinfo.com